Strategies for
Secondary Teachers

This book is dedicated to Fritz Bell,
my mentor, my friend, my inspiration for over 32 years.

I would also like to acknowledge Jeffery Sullivan for
all his help, support, and encouragement through the writing process.

RTI

Strategies for Secondary Teachers

SUSAN GINGRAS FITZELL

CORWIN
A SAGE Company

CORWIN
A SAGE Company

FOR INFORMATION:

Corwin
A SAGE Company
2455 Teller Road
Thousand Oaks, California 91320
(800) 233-9936
Fax: (800) 417-2466
www.corwin.com

SAGE Ltd.
1 Oliver's Yard
55 City Road
London EC1Y 1SP
United Kingdom

SAGE India Pvt. Ltd.
B 1/I 1 Mohan Cooperative Industrial Area
Mathura Road, New Delhi 110 044
India

SAGE Asia-Pacific Pte. Ltd.
33 Pekin Street #02-01
Far East Square
Singapore 048763

Acquisitions Editor: Jessica Allan
Associate Editor: Allison Scott
Editorial Assistant: Lisa Whitney
Production Editor: Veronica Stapleton
Copy Editor: Alan Cook
Typesetter: C&M Digitals (P) Ltd.
Proofreader: Christine Dahlin
Indexer: Sheila Bodell
Cover Designer: Michael Dubowe
Permissions Editor: Karen Ehrmann
Figure Designer: Catherine Laplace

Printed in the United States of America.

Library of Congress Cataloging-in-Publication Data

Fitzell, Susan Gingras.
RTI strategies for secondary teachers / Susan Gingras Fitzell.

p. cm.
Includes bibliographical references and index.

ISBN 978-1-4129-9222-0 (pbk.)

1. Reading—Remedial teaching. 2. Reading (Middle school) 3. Reading (Secondary) I. Title.

LB1050.5.F549 2011
428.4071'2—dc22
2011011496

This book is printed on acid-free paper.

11 12 13 14 15 10 9 8 7 6 5 4 3 2 1

Contents

Preface

For teachers, the day rarely ends with the last school bell of the day. Lesson plans and concerns about students linger in the mind beyond the classroom. "If I could just . . . , but will it work?" "Will I lose ground in teaching the concept?" "Is it too risky?" "Will it help my students make the grade, pass the state tests, or get into college?" "Will my students resist out-of-the-box methods?"

Research-based classroom strategies are strategies for which there is "Yes, it works!" data. Even when armed with statistics that show the efficacy of best practice teaching methods, teachers still ask, "How do I do it?" As a teachers' coach, I often hear, "It would be so good to have a strategy bank to refer to when I need ideas and techniques for the classroom." This book, *RTI Strategies for Secondary Teachers,* fills that request.

The research presented in this text is the most up-to-date educational research available. Unfortunately, it seems that once it has been shown that a given method meets the criteria for the title of "best practice," continuing research on that teaching method comes to a halt. Although the research on those methods may be older, they are still effective strategies. As a response to this phenomenon, this text presents an explanation of single-subject experimental design.

This book is written for teachers. As it stands, some readers might find that the research included in each lesson plan distracts from the goal of the book. Research is critical to Response to Intervention (RTI) and must be included. However, my approach to research is just as practical and realistic as my approach to teaching. I did not get hung up on overtheorizing and overresearching. Teachers want solutions, not theory.

Chapter 1 pertains to RTI overall, its efficacy, and the evidence supporting its use in secondary education. It includes examples of how some schools and teachers have mitigated the budgeting, staffing, performance, and student culture constraints faced at the secondary level.

Each subsequent chapter provides at least two strategies, presented in sample lesson plans, related to its title. Each chapter begins with a short explanation of why these particular strategies were selected for this book, the research that demonstrates their effectiveness, and detailed instructions on how to implement the lessons and extension activities. All three tiers are addressed in each lesson plan, so that the reader has a model of what RTI looks like in the classroom.

The final chapter explains acceleration centers, a process that incorporates many of the strategies presented in the previous chapters. Teachers who develop these low-maintenance acceleration centers will always have a set of meaningful learning activities readily available and will know that they meet both the interests and needs of their students.

While the main contribution this book makes to the teaching professional is a bank of research-proven RTI strategies that will improve state test score results and student achievement, there are several other benefits. Implementing RTI strategies supports *all* of our students, not just our struggling learners.

The grouping strategies inherent in each lesson plan improve the social skills of our student populations and may, depending on other circumstances, reduce the need for special education outside the main classroom. Essentially, my hope is that this book raises teaching up a level in every classroom and reduces stress for teachers and students in the process.

Acknowledgments

Corwin gratefully acknowledges the contributions of the following contributors:

Sally Jean Coghlan
RSP Eighth-Grade Special Education Teacher and Site Department Chair
Rio Linda Junior High School
Twin Rivers Unified School District
Rio Linda, CA

Wendy Dallman
Special Education Teacher
New London High School
New London, WI

Jolene Dockstader
Seventh-Grade Language Arts Teacher
Jerome Middle School
Jerome, ID

JoAnn Hiatt
Math Teacher
Olathe East High School
Olathe, KS

Susan Kessler
Executive Principal
Hunters Lane High School
Nashville, TN

Karen Tichy
Associate Superintendent
Catholic Education Office
Archdiocese of St. Louis
Catholic Education Office
St. Louis, MO

About the Author

Susan Gingras Fitzell, M. Ed., has been touching lives in public schools and beyond since 1980. She has over three decades of experience identifying and meeting the needs of youth with special needs, those who have behavioral and anger management issues, and students who experience bullying. Susan's work focuses on building caring, inclusive school communities and helping students and teachers succeed in the inclusive classroom.

Susan is a dynamic, nationally recognized presenter and educational consultant specializing in special education and Response to Intervention topics, co-teaching, bullying prevention, and adolescent anger management. She provides practical strategies to increase achievement of all students in all classrooms. Susan's motto is "Good for all; critical for students who learn differently."

Susan's greatest satisfaction comes from helping teachers make a positive impact using practical, doable strategies that fuel positive, measurable results. Whether she's doing a one-day workshop or long-term consulting, Susan's straightforward, commonsense approach always yields positive results.

Other books by Susan Fitzell:

Free the Children: Conflict Educational for Strong Peaceful Minds (1997)

Special Needs in the General Classroom: Strategies That Make It Work (2004)

Transforming Anger to Personal Power: An Anger Management Curriculum for Grades 6 Through 12 (2004)

Please Help Me With My Homework! Strategies for Parents and Caregivers (2005)

Umm . . . Studying? What's That? Learning Strategies for the Overwhelmed and Confused College and High School Student (2006; coauthored with her daughter, Shivahn Fitzell)

Susan is available for in-service training and consultation and for keynote presentations.

For free educational resources and a video sample of Susan's presentations, go to her website at www.susanfitzell.com.

For more information, contact Susan at sfitzell@susanfitzell.com.

1

Introduction

Why This Book This Way?

This book is for the classroom teacher and intervention specialist. Its purpose is to alleviate classroom teacher stress and confusion regarding RTI at the secondary level. Response to Intervention could also be called "responding to the struggling learner with academic interventions that match the student's needs." Often, intervention teams struggle with the question, "Now that we understand Johnny's difficulty in the classroom, what positive strategy can we use to effectively support Johnny's learning?" Seeking and sorting out strategies is time-consuming.

This text focuses on building an intervention bank of Tiers One, Two, and Three interventions for Grades 6 through 12. Most books presently available on RTI explain the process, how to set up intervention teams, how to get buy-in, and how to do the research. These books address Response to Intervention from a systemic standpoint. What's missing is a clear summary of RTI in teacher-friendly language. Also currently lacking are easily implemented, practical, research-based interventions for secondary classroom teachers to employ.

Team members truly want to help students be successful, but are often at a loss as to which teaching strategy will work best. There is no one-size-fits-all solution to every learning difficulty. If intervention team members had a guide that provided potential solutions, the team would have a starting place. My goal is for this book to serve as that guide.

By providing practical, research-based strategies for interventions and example lesson plans from Tier One through Tier Three, my hope is that teachers will gain a solid understanding of how to take any lesson plan, whether old or new, and adjust it to address all three tiers.

I have taken well-known lesson plans, reformatted them to include the three tiers of RTI, and included rubrics for progress monitoring. However, I have also included novel, lesser-known interventions to provoke the reader into thinking outside the box. Many outstanding strategies are cast aside or ignored at the secondary level because they appear "elementary" to some. An intervention should be judged by its effectiveness, not its appearance. The strategies and examples offered here have all been used, with positive results, at the secondary level.

Also, the sample lesson plans in this book provide a visual model for teachers to use as a resource. These examples show how a teacher might take any lesson plan and adapt it for RTI by using familiar concepts.

■ EDUCATIONAL JARGON AND THIS BOOK

There are several challenges to writing a text that is both research-based and uses language that fosters the credibility of the text, yet does not get jargon-based and so academic that we lose the reader. The ordinary, everyday language used in this book does not diminish the content of the underlying research. Quite the contrary, it makes it easier for teachers to use this work as a strategy bank by using the common language that we might speak in the classroom when working with our students.

■ SOME REDUNDANCY

As we know, many students who struggle in school or do not respond to instruction have common deficits. Consequently, many of the lesson plans address the same learner needs. Each lesson plan includes a section titled *Addresses These Nonresponder Indicators*. My intent with this section is to assist teachers in determining which challenges that lesson plan might address. Consequently, there is some redundancy in this section throughout the book. Because many teachers may not read every lesson plan and will simply choose which ones they want to use, I erred on the side of repetition. For example, many lessons address

- Attention Deficit Disorder;
- difficulty connecting new information with previously learned knowledge;
- struggle to effectively use words to express organized and complete thoughts in writing; and
- below-standard word usage skills.

Their recurrence in the lessons is deliberate and allows each sample lesson plan to stand alone.

This book is a tool for you as a teacher to use in your efforts to reach all learners in your classroom and an opportunity for you to open your mind to new and exciting ideas in your quest for good teaching.

Figure 1.1   Like the Cogs of an Engine, the Characteristics of Good Teaching Propel Each Other

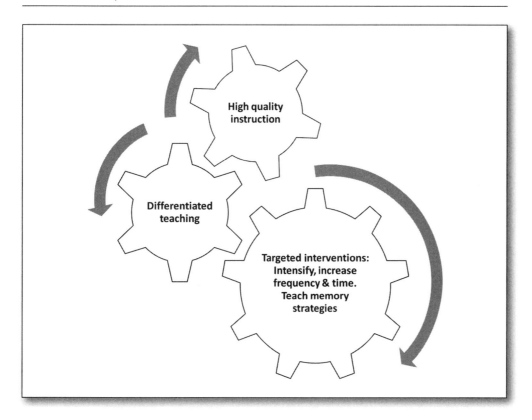

2

A Snapshot of the Response to Intervention Process

■ **THE THREE TIERS (SOMETIMES FOUR)**

"RTI is the practice of providing high quality instruction/intervention matched to students' needs and using learning rate over time and the level of performance to make important educational decisions to guide instruction" (National Reading Panel, 2000, p. 87).

Because Response to Intervention is typically considered a three-tier model, this book operates on that premise. However, some school districts and states, such as Georgia, employ a four-tier model (Bender & Shores, 2007). Most of the literature on Response to Intervention does not refer to Tier Four.

Let's review the three-tier model: Tier One of RTI requires consistent high quality classroom instruction that incorporates three nonnegotiable components:

1. A standards-based core curriculum
2. Differentiating instruction so that all students can learn
3. A variety of authentic assessments geared to monitoring student progress and guiding instruction.

TIER ONE ■

Tier One of RTI requires the use of best practice, research-based teaching methods. As Robert Marzano discusses in *Dimensions of Learning* (Marzano, Pickering, & Pollock, 2001), research-based strategies implemented in the differentiated classroom reduce the need for interventions.

My experience teaching at the high school level as both a special education teacher and a co-teacher working within the inclusion model, as well as my experience coaching in middle and high schools around the country, convinces me that every secondary classroom needs to begin at Tier One: differentiating instruction so that all students can learn.

Differentiated instruction is teaching to different learning preferences and using a variety of teaching methods to reach all students. It sometimes encompasses using multiple levels of instruction during the same lesson plan. Examples might include using materials at three different reading levels so that all students can read, having two or three choices of activities based on multiple intelligences, or having three levels of a test. Essentially, differentiating instruction means using a variety of methods in any lesson plan to reach all learners. When teachers differentiate instruction, 80% to 90% of students successfully meet achievement benchmarks (Hanson, 2009). Consider the following realities:

- The verbal, linguistic, auditory delivery of information, in which students are expected to passively sit in their seats and absorb information while copying notes at rapid speed, does not work for all students.
- The students it does not work for are those who do not respond well to education and are doing poorly in the classroom as well as on state tests. While this method may work for some teachers and students, it is unproductive for the majority of our struggling student population.
- A consequence of the lack of differentiation at the secondary level is that students who move on to college, whether to engineering coursework or a technical school, primarily know only one mode of studying. When they become college students and meet challenging coursework, they may lack the study skills they need in the more rigorous academic environment. This is why our most successful high school students sometimes do not meet expectations at the college level.

> The reality is that until we differentiate instruction at the secondary level, a basic requirement of Tier One RTI, we are shortchanging all our students: English language learners, students with special needs, trade-bound students, and students heading off to college.

How do we differentiate instruction?

- By using teaching strategies that support all intelligence styles and modes of learning, as well as challenging ourselves to implement center activities such as Fitzell Acceleration Centers™, station teaching, and flexible grouping within our pedagogy.

- By not trying to cover it all, but instead looking critically at the standards-based core curriculum and focus on what is most important, thereby allowing time for meaningful teaching, repetition, and student practice.
- By incorporating multiple modes of assessment. RTI requires authentic assessments—a variety of measures that clearly identify what the student knows and what the student does not know.

Again, the most important concept to take away from this chapter is that Response to Intervention is simply "Really Terrific Instruction. . ."

There are times when students will fail to learn despite the best efforts of the teacher. Master teachers who differentiate instruction and respond to student needs still encounter students who struggle to learn the content required by the curriculum. As teachers take note of the student who is failing to respond to the teaching methodology, they need to consider how to reapproach the subject and intervene so that students will become successful.

■ TIER TWO

Using curriculum-based measurement practices, teachers determine where the student is lacking and then seek Tier Two interventions that might be appropriate for that student. Often, Tier Two interventions can be research-based practices used in Tier One, but with three modifications:

1. Specific students receive more intense instruction and application of the strategies.

2. Students are given more time to practice and implement the strategies.

3. The intensity of implementation may increase.

It may be appropriate, at times, to provide Tier Two interventions in a flexible grouping situation in the general classroom. This may prevent students from being pulled out of the classroom, which would cause them to miss critical instruction (Wright, 2007).

If teachers routinely implemented small group work, flexible grouping, or center teaching, then interventions in Tier Two would fall right into place in the lesson plan.

Having adequate time to implement interventions is often the greatest challenge faced at the secondary level. When students need more intervention than can be provided within the general classroom, they should receive an additional class for Tier Two interventions. If the time is not available during standard school hours, the interventions need to be provided outside of the school day. Typically, students are encouraged or required to attend after-school tutoring programs so that Tier Two interventions may be implemented.

An option that works well for students at the secondary level (Grades 6 through 12) is a tutored study hall. This is neither a resource room nor a special education resource; it is a study hall where content-area teachers, specialists, or support staff are available to implement interventions. This class can be built into the students' schedules just as a study hall would be. Ideally, the content-area teachers engage in professional development, mentoring, or team learning that supports their efforts in implementing those strategies in the classroom. Providing students with additional instructional time that incorporates intervention strategies increases the possibility that they ultimately will be successful (Shores & Chester, 2009).

At the elementary level, many teachers use published programs providing intervention solutions available to them. Although these published programs are highly touted and profitable for publishing companies, they are not the panacea some would like to believe. However, they provide a level of comfort to school districts trying to implement Response to Intervention because these programs are often scripted and are very clear about what to do to address a student's difficulties. Rarely are these programs available at the secondary level. Scripted middle school and junior high math programs are one of the few exceptions.

This is better for students and teachers in the long term. Rather than forcing teachers to follow a script from a published program, teachers are encouraged to use their professional skills, experience, and an understanding of student needs in order to determine appropriate interventions. Teachers simply use a problem-solving model to hone in on possible interventions.

TIER THREE ■

Tier Three is not as delineated as Tiers One and Two in literature on Response to Intervention. School districts define Tier Three requirements as follows:

- Interventions are more intensive, based on problem-solving models, and implemented through a combination of means including classroom instruction, outside-of-school instruction, or in-school instruction outside of the general classroom.
- A combination of intensive interventions implemented in general education as part of a wrap-around approach to meeting a student's needs.
- Some school districts, as well as books on the topic of RTI, consider special education to be part of Tier Three.

In this book, Tier Three interventions are considered part of the general education process that is implemented before students may be referred for special education services. Tier Three is neither a place nor a program. It is a level of intervention services. Once a student is identified as being able to benefit from special needs services, that student is no longer considered part of the Response to Intervention protocol. "In most schools, Tier Three is not special education but is more intensive intervention to try to improve the progress and avoid the necessity of placement in special education" (Hall, 2008, p. 68).

Tier Three is the most intensive phase of the RTI three-tier system. At Tier Three, students receive intervention instruction with greater frequency, with more intensity, and for a longer time. Students who have not responded to Tier One or Tier Two efforts and who have significant difficulty being successful in the general curriculum might receive one-to-one, one-to-two, or small group intensive instruction.

At the secondary level, Tier Three interventions pose the greatest challenge for implementation.

At the elementary level, Tier Three would typically incorporate two 30-minute intervention periods every day. This schedule is logistically challenging, if not impossible, at the middle and high school levels. Intervention teams must think outside the box in order to come up with realistic intervention schedules.

General classroom teachers will rarely have time to implement Tier Three interventions, but may instead choose to use intervention strategies in their lesson plans in the following ways:

- Intervention strategies are implemented by specialists, tutors, and support staff.
- Instructional labs are set up as part of the school schedule.
- Often, intervention schedules at the secondary level for Tier Two and Three must be implemented outside of the school day.

Here again is where the role of the general education teacher is critical. At the secondary level, much can be accomplished in the general education classroom if the teacher is (1) incorporating differentiated instruction strategies in the classroom, (2) making an effort to incorporate interventions for specific students in lesson plans so that all students might also benefit, and (3) willing to use a variety of research-based strategies as a means of scaffolding to support student learning outcomes.

If the secondary general education teacher is also willing to implement flexible grouping and center teaching such as Fitzell Acceleration Centers to support the learning process, many interventions can be supported, enhanced, and implemented directly in the classroom.

■ HOW DOES RTI FIT INTO A SECONDARY EDUCATION MODEL?

There is very little research on implementation of Response to Intervention at the secondary level (Shores & Chester, 2009). RTI was initially implemented as an early intervention program focusing on literacy at the lower elementary level. It is becoming increasingly apparent, however, that schools need to address students who are not successful in Grades 6 through 12 with something other than the traditional pattern of referring them to special education.

Some consider Response to Intervention to be primarily a pullout or after-school initiative. This pullout approach is difficult to implement at the secondary level because

- pullouts for a particular subject area should not take place during the class time regularly scheduled for that subject: Pullouts for English interventions should not be during English class, and pullouts for math interventions should not be during math class. An intervention requires extra time, not replacement time.
- schools are short-staffed and lack after-school resources and time;
- it is difficult to find a class from which students can be pulled in order to implement an intervention plan;
- at the middle school level, a pullout program often requires a student to be pulled from his or her exploratory classes, thereby causing the student to miss valuable hands-on learning experiences; and
- at the high school level, students with a study hall could be pulled for interventions. However, this requires that a teacher be available to implement the intervention during that period.

Other effective options include

- implementing RTI in the general classroom by the general education teacher or a co-teaching team; and
- using a push-in model that takes advantage of the skill sets of specialists (for example, speech pathologists, occupational therapists, and intervention specialists).

> Interventions then become, primarily, the responsibility of the general classroom teacher. The advantage to this approach is that all students benefit from the use of best practices, thereby making overall classroom teaching that much more effective.

GENERAL EDUCATION VERSUS SPECIAL EDUCATION AND RESPONSIBLE INCLUSION ■

You may be questioning whether students who need Tier Three interventions, and in some cases Tier Two interventions, should be in the general classroom as opposed to receiving special education services. Because some districts and authors are calling Tier Three "special education," there are two schools of thought. After co-teaching in inclusive classrooms and witnessing the benefits of inclusion done well in schools and school districts around the country, I am convinced that most students achieve more in the general classroom with an environment of excellent teaching.

A small percentage of students are best served within the framework of special education and special classrooms. However, the reality is that this is a small group. In many school districts, special education caseloads are overwhelming. If we properly implement RTI, we allow special education teachers to work more intensely with the students who have the greatest needs.

Response to Intervention provides general educators with the tools to reach most learners while allowing special educators to more effectively meet the needs of the student with special needs.

With a system for Response to Intervention in place, secondary teachers can provide instruction that reaches a variety of learning styles, gives additional time where necessary, and monitors progress. The classroom teacher adjusts interventions based on student performance, as determined by progress monitoring. With RTI, classroom teaching is data driven and differentiated.

RTI calls upon teachers to break away from the traditional mode of verbal linguistic and auditory teaching, especially at the middle and high school levels. It embraces differentiated instruction that responds to varying student learning styles. Teachers will get the satisfaction of seeing students become more successful than they ever imagined because they intervened with student-centered strategies.

The High School Tiered Interventions Initiative (HSTII) is a partnership between The National High School Center, the National Center on Response to Intervention, and the Center on Instruction. The initiative's focus is to find secondary RTI models currently implemented, to ascertain what might work or not work with those models, and define the key characteristics of best practices at the secondary level.

Because there is no textbook model currently available for implementation of RTI at the secondary level, there is no *one* way to implement the process. It is up to school districts to figure out how best to meet the needs of their learners.

I recently interviewed several school districts to see where they were in the RTI implementation process. The following are examples of RTI strategies in place.

Community High School District 155 of Illinois has an RTI team composed of teachers, counselors, psychologists, building administrators, principals, and vice-principals. Still in the early stages of RTI development, they began the process in a logical place: establishing a strong foundation at Tier One. All secondary teachers in the district receive extensive training in differentiating instruction. The expectation is that those teachers will implement differentiated instruction in their classrooms daily. With a solid footing at Tier One, they are developing Tier Two; yet, they did not leave Tier One behind. They continue to improve upon Tier One, researching high quality best practices and exploring co-teaching. An important step they took was to research measurement and data collection options to identify a fitting measurement device for the many initiatives already implemented.

Southland Independent School District in Texas also has an RTI team in place, which includes an administrator, a reading specialist, and a dyslexia coordinator. At Tier One, all teachers regularly differentiate instruction. At Tier Two, general education teachers use flexible grouping three times a week. They also implement peer tutoring. At Tier Three, middle school students are pulled from their noncore classes for interventions that support core classes.

Southland utilizes a variety of tools to complement their RTI plan. The following are highlights of these tools:

- AIMSweb (http://www.aimsweb.com) is used to perform diagnostic assessment and progress monitoring.
- Read Naturally (http://www.readnaturally.com) supports students' Tier Three fluency and comprehension needs.
- Kent State University professor of literacy Tim Rasinski's set of high-fluency phrases provides both an assessment tool and an intervention. The high-fluency phases are words that students will frequently encounter when reading. The students are encouraged to read the sheet as fast as they can, and to repeat the process for practice.

- Every Day Edits (http://www.educationworld.com) is a site that builds language skills, increases test scores, and improves cultural literacy. Students are given a short paragraph with ten errors in it. As a Tier Three intervention strategy, the students practice finding and correcting the errors. This causes the students to ask a question about what it is that makes errors wrong, which leads to a teaching opportunity and deeper understanding.
- Minimystery CDs, which can be listened to by students while reading along. After listening to the story, the students answer a question, which assesses their reading comprehension and critical thinking abilities.

Southland's eighth graders achieved a 100% passing rate on their state tests in 2010. Teachers feel this was a direct result of the RTI process. It is interesting to note that at Southland, none of the students receiving Tier Three interventions are students with special needs. They don't even have a special education teacher on the RTI team.

Havana High School of *Havana Community Unit School District 126 (Illinois)* employs the mantra *Every Child, Every Day,* and says they are at the "What do we need now?" stage of RTI implementation.

The sole high school in the district, Havana has only 350 students. Their RTI team consists of a social worker, a psychologist, a teacher, the principal, a school counselor, and an RTI specialist.

All teachers are expected to differentiate. Every freshman is assigned an adult mentor who checks in with the student every day.

If a student is earning lower than a C, the RTI team and the student's mentor pull the student's grades and meet with the student to discuss his or her learning. Consequently, no student slips through the cracks. Someone is always checking in with each student.

If a student is failing a class, or in danger of failing a class, then that student is assigned to Academic Learning Support, a structured study hall. A skilled paraprofessional monitors the study hall room for the entire day at Havana. The paraprofessional has a list of students receiving RTI team assistance. Instead of covering a study hall, teachers are now available during that time for academic assistance.

As a Tier Three intervention, Havana High offers struggling readers a reading class, which counts as an elective. Students in the class receive direct reading instruction from the teacher, read novels, and use LEXIA reading software (http://www.lexialearning.com). Students who are struggling in math can take a double-block math class, which provides them with one math credit and one elective credit.

The administration is changing the evaluation system for professional development so that it focuses more on teacher instruction.

Midland High School of *Midland Community School District 7 (Illinois)* is in the early stages of RTI development. Their RTI teams include co-teaching teams from the English and math departments as well as the principal. The entire teaching staff is expected to differentiate instruction at Tier One regardless of whether students are receiving RTI interventions.

Midland is using The Key to Tracker learning assessment software (http://www.keypress.com) to monitor students' learning progress. The co-teaching team divides their block-scheduled class, with two 20-minute interventions scheduled into each two-hour block, one at the beginning of the period and one at the end. Each intervention session targets a different set of students. There is an intense focus on the freshman class because being successful as a freshman sets a student up for three more years of success.

These school districts differ drastically in their process and progress. Any one of them could serve as a model for a starting point at your school or in your district. My goal in sharing these vignettes is to reinforce the message that, at this point in time, there is no one right way to implement RTI at the secondary level. I recently worked with a high school that believed they were making a mess of RTI. I disagreed. The school diligently worked at assessing what they already had in place, evaluating next steps, and bringing in support to help them move forward. That's a positive start.

Start the process, assess, adjust, and reassess. Most important, once the process is started, support teachers and intervention specialists with hands-on examples of how to plan lessons for RTI.

■ ASSESSMENT? WELL, I QUIZ EVERY FRIDAY . . .

How we assess students to determine their understanding of content is critical to the Response to Intervention process. Schools are becoming more and more locked into using

- summative assessment;
- standardized measures of student achievement;
- multiple-choice tests; and
- other traditional forms of written assessment.

> Although teachers may use these methods because these are the measures required for state testing, it is truly an inaccurate, and I would argue an unethical, means of evaluating students.

The only true evaluation is authentic assessment. Authentic assessments incorporate a variety of measures into the evaluation process and focus on formative assessment. Types of authentic assessment include

- rubrics;
- exit cards;
- curriculum-based measurement;
- student self-evaluation; and
- documented observations.

> When assessing with a variety of measures, teachers build a portfolio of data that provides a more accurate picture of the student as a learner. With this authentic, data-driven student portrait, teachers have the necessary information to do the problem-solving and detective work required for determining appropriate interventions.

For example, when students draw what they've learned (a nonlinguistic learning strategy), the teacher can walk around the room holding an observation record sheet and assess student understanding by looking at their drawings and asking questions for clarification. Documenting those observations will provide a form of authentic and immediate ongoing assessment.

In RTI, three types of assessments are used for three different purposes: universal screening, diagnostics, and progress monitoring.

Universal Screening

Universal screening is used to determine which students need closer monitoring, differentiated instruction, or a specific intervention (three or more times a year). Resources for universal screening include

- AIMSweb through Grade 8
- EdCheckup through Grade 8
- STEEP—http://www.isteep.com/datatools.html#prod—through Grade 12:
  - Middle school oral reading fluency and maze (comprehension)
  - High school oral reading fluency and maze
  - Secondary math concepts and application fundamentals
- http://www.thinkgate.net/ (a framework for setting up assessments)
- Alternate screening tools at the high school level:
  - Grades—failing core academics (especially freshmen)
  - Analyze attendance records for student absences: Missed 10 of the first 30 days of school
  - Identifying students who are overage for their grade level
  - State standardized assessments

Diagnostics

Diagnostics determine what students can and cannot do in important academic areas. Diagnostic assessments can include preassessments, measures of a student's prior knowledge, baseline data, documented observations, or probing questions to assess student understanding.

Progress Monitoring

Progress monitoring is simply assessing a student's progress on an ongoing basis as opposed to assessing at the end of a unit or in a manner that does not allow teachers to catch students before they fail. As a means to monitor progress, teachers use quick one- to three-minute assessments several times per week to determine if it's appropriate to move forward with instruction, reteach to the whole group, or reteach to a few (see table). It's a step above the pop quiz because rather than just using the quiz data to enter a grade for students, the data is used to drive instruction.

Progress Monitoring Versus What We Have Done Historically

Traditional Assessments	Progress Monitoring
• Typically lengthy and time-consuming • Administered infrequently or at the end of a unit • Typically, students do not receive immediate feedback • Feedback may not inform instructional planning	• Easy and quick method for gathering student performance data • Administered frequently • Students and teachers receive immediate feedback to adjust instruction • Students are compared to peers and local norms

Following are some common methods of progress monitoring:

Curriculum-Based Measurement (CBM)

Curriculum-based measurement is one form of a scientifically based method for monitoring progress. CBMs describe academic competence, track academic development, and improve student achievement. The three purposes of CBMs are screening, progress monitoring, and instructional diagnosis.

Rubrics

Rubrics are performance-based assessment tools used to evaluate student performance on a task, a set of tasks, or a learning outcome. Rubrics use specific criteria, in the form of narrative descriptions, as a basis for evaluating student performance. Most rubrics use a tabular format that identifies the level of student achievement, from low-to-high or high-to-low, based upon the proficiency that the student is able to achieve. Rating scales may be numerical, qualitative, or both.

The sample lesson plans in this text employ rubrics in order to clearly illustrate performance goals and assist in identifying the level of intervention necessary for different students with each activity. They are also a valid example of a progress-monitoring tool.

Exit Cards

Exit cards are a simple assessment tool. Each card will have a set of just two or three questions for students to answer after you teach a lesson. Students answer the questions before the bell rings. It is the last thing they do in class. They must hand the card to the teacher before they walk out the door, hence the name *exit cards*. It's ongoing, immediate assessment in action. Exit cards (a.k.a. *tickets to leave*) are used to gather information on student readiness levels, understanding of concepts just taught, interests, and learning profiles.

Exit cards can be used to form intervention pairs, triads, and groups.

After a lesson, use exit cards to assess student understanding or interest. Keep the items on the cards short and to the point. Keep it simple!

When reviewing the cards that are implemented as an assessment tool, score them with a 1 if the student does not understand the concept, got the answer wrong, or needs reteaching. Score them with a 2 if the student understands but needs more practice. Score them with a 3 if the student understands the concept and is ready to move on (see Figure 2.1).

Then use the cards to group students.

You might put all the students who received a 1 together and reteach that group (or small groups). Put those who received a 2 together (or in small groups) and give them a practice activity. Put those who got a 3 together and assign them an enrichment activity, or an investigation.

Alternatively, you might put a 1, a 2, and a 3 together in a triad to practice the skill (see Figure 2.2).

Other possible uses for the data from the exit cards are to determine student interest or strengths in a topic or to group students by learning style. (see Figure 2.3).

Grouping by student or interest is another option that might be explored by using exit cards to determine a student's preferred learning style, interests, and strengths (see Figure 2.4).

Examples of possible exit cards are shown in Figures 2.6 (see page 19) and 2.7 (see page 20). It might even be more effective to simplify the questions to a greater degree. The exit cards shown in Figure 2.6 (see page 19) could be broken up into four exit cards rather than two. The key is knowing your goal. What do you want the exit card to show? Keep it simple and effective.

Additional quick assessments might include:

- High-fluency phrases from *The Fluent Reader* by Timothy V. Rasinski (Rasknski, 2003). Do an Internet search on a paper titled "Phrases and Short Sentences for Repeated Reading Practice."
- Every-Day Edits are also effective as both an assessment and an intervention. Search for Every-Day Edits at http://www.educationalworld.com.

Figure 2.1   Exit Card Grouping: Mixed-Ability Level Triads

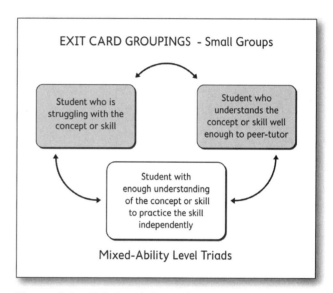

Figure 2.2   Exit Card Grouping: Ability Level Groups

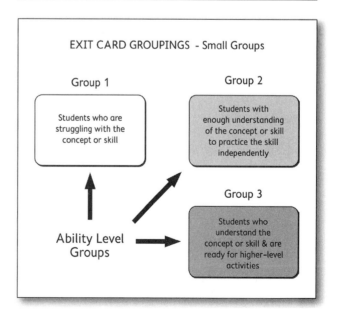

Figure 2.3   Exit Card Grouping: Content Differentiated Groups

Figure 2.4   Exit Card Grouping: Interest or Process Groups

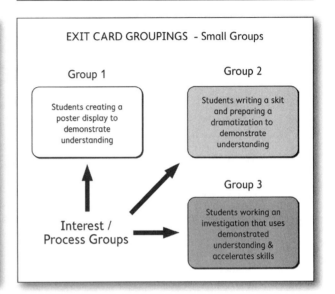

■ RESEARCH-BASED STRATEGIES INCORPORATED IN THIS BOOK

The requirement to use only research-based strategies for interventions initially troubled me. Having spent years teaching and working directly with students, whether one on one or within inclusive classrooms, I conclude that there are successful strategies that are used with students that do not have a research study to back them up. To assume that a strategy or method is not effective simply because one cannot find a study to validate its use seems disrespectful of many teachers' skills—skills that rely upon their good judgment. Consequently, I investigated the concept of acceptable research and in doing so discovered *single-subject experimental design.*

Learning about single-subject experimental design alleviated my angst. I could use a strategy that I knew worked for many of the students that I and others have taught over the years, as long as I collected data and used the protocol for single-subject experimental design. *"Single subject experimental designs involve evaluation of a single person or a small group before, during, and following the implementation of the intervention. Single subject experimental designs control for threats to the internal validity of the study"* (Brown-Chidsey & Steege, 2005, p. 40; emphasis added). An excellent resource that provides a clear explanation of the process for single-subject research design is *Response to Intervention: Principles and Strategies for Effective Practice* by Rachel Brown-Chidsey and Mark W. Steege. Chapter 5 of that book explains single-subject experimental design well.

Most of the interventions referred to in this book have their research base documented in two sources: *Classroom Instruction That Works* (Marzano et al., 2001) and *A Mind at a Time* (Levine, 2003). I am pleased that because of the excellent work of these two authors I can go to one book for most of my academic research and another book for research on how memory works and impacts learners. These two texts are not the only sources for research, however, in my efforts to keep it simple for the reader, it makes sense to me to cite the texts that present the most research in one place and in an easy-to-read format.

ALL RIGHT! IF I *HAVE* TO DO THIS, ■
WHAT DO I *REALLY* HAVE TO DO? AND HOW?

Keep reading this book and you will be told, in teacher-friendly language, how to implement RTI easily, with many practical, research-based Tier One, Tier Two, and Tier Three Interventions for secondary classrooms.

The sample lesson plans provided in this text model ways to adapt any lesson plan in your current curriculum to the three tiers of intervention. It is hoped that the reader will be challenged to rethink long-held myths about what is appropriate at the high school level. Many high school students are denied effective learning tools simply because they "look" elementary, even though research and practice say otherwise.

Every strategy in this book begins at Tier One as a differentiated instruction strategy. Then I demonstrate how it might be used at Tiers Two and Three in a typical lesson plan. Consider the three-tier chart that follows.

**Lesson Plan Application to
Response to Intervention Tiers**

Tier One	Tier Two	Tier Three
Teacher introduces the lesson to the entire class using a variety of strategies to differentiate instruction.	Students apply specific learning strategies within the content area to internalize the skill by working with a peer tutor, a specialist, or in a coaching session with the classroom teacher. Tier Two interventions are implemented at least twice per week until the study strategy is mastered.	Students work with a specialist one on one for an additional 60 to 90 minutes per week, using this intervention as a strategy to facilitate proficiency.

When breaking down each sample lesson plan, one might visualize the three tiers as illustrated in this chart. The lesson plans indicate what strategies are to be used at each tier, essentially meeting the guidelines presented in the chart.

At the secondary level, it is important for students to make these strategies their own. Consequently, strategies are presented as they might be used by the teacher, as well as by students.

OPTIONS FOR DETERMINING WHICH ■
STUDENTS SHOULD BE IN WHICH GROUPS

All of the lesson plan samples in this text include group work or paired learning. There are several methods teachers can use to form groups. Assessment data can be used; for example, teachers might use standardized test scores, curriculum-based measurement, progress monitoring, or informal assessments such as classroom observations, exit cards, action research, observation, and student self-assessment.

Teachers might also group students based on targeted areas of instruction. Students doing poorly on a specific state standard or struggling to understand a curriculum concept might be grouped together to accelerate growth or to deliver an intervention.

Students might also be grouped in mixed-ability groups, so that in every group there are peer tutors and supports in place for students who are struggling. Sometimes we may simply want pairs. The diagram below demonstrates the High with Middle, Middle with Low method of pairing students. Sort your class roster by grades, then divide the class in half and pair students as illustrated. This process ensures that you never pair the highest student with the lowest and provides different pairs each week, based on student averages (see Figure 2.5).

Figure 2.5 High With Middle, Middle With Low Grouping Technique

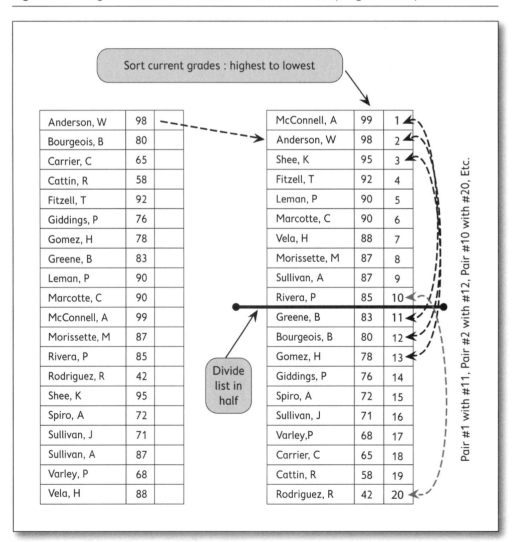

Figure 2.6 Exit Card Examples

Name: _____ Date: _____

Today, you began to learn about _____
List three things you learned:

1. _____

2. _____

3. _____

Write at least one question you have about this topic.

_____

_____

_____

Name: _____ Date: _____

Today, you began to learn about _____

What area gave you the most difficulty today?

_____

_____

Something that helped me in my learning today was:

_____

_____

_____

Figure 2.7   More Exit Card Examples

Name: _____ Date: _____

Explain the difference between _____ and

_____. Give some examples of each as part of your explanation.

_____

_____

_____

_____

_____

_____

Name: _____ Date: _____

We used the following learning strategies in this lesson:

1. _____

2. _____

3. _____

What learning strategy or strategies seemed to work best for you?

_____

_____

_____

3

Vocabulary Intervention Strategies

USE VOCABULARY MAPPING TO ACQUIRE NEW VOCABULARY ■

Vocabulary mapping is a familiar strategy for many educators at all grade levels. I'm a firm believer in mapping strategies, and there is an abundance of research to support mind mapping and graphic organizers. The typical vocabulary map has students write a definition, synonym, and sentence as well as draw a picture.

I've varied the strategy slightly to incorporate humor with the "silly sentence" because the brain remembers humor. I have also incorporated stem words with the definition. When students learn the stem or root meaning of words, they are more apt to expand that understanding to new vocabulary. My goal when creating a lesson plan is to layer as many strategies as possible in the same block of time to reach students with a variety of learning styles in the shortest amount of time. For example, rather than spend 15 minutes on a lesson using the auditory mode of delivery, I'd prefer to use multiple modes of delivery in that same 15 minutes to deliver the equivalent amount of instruction. Again, time constraints at the secondary level must be considered when implementing RTI.

Research Background

David W. Moore and John E. Readence suggest that gains in vocabulary knowledge following graphic organizer use may be even greater than gains in comprehension. The average effect size for the 23 studies reviewed was more than twice as large as that reported for comprehension, indicating that graphic organizers are a very effective tool for improving vocabulary knowledge (Moore & Readence, 1984).

Learning Objectives

- To acquire new vocabulary
- To connect that vocabulary to themes and categories
- To use appropriate questioning to gather information

Addresses These Nonresponder Indicators

- The student has Attention Deficit Disorder or an auditory learning deficit.
- The student has difficulty connecting new information with previously learned knowledge.
- The student has difficulty processing information in a way that is meaningful to him or her.
- The student has difficulty recoding incoming information into meaningful information.
- The student has reading comprehension difficulties in which vocabulary affects understanding and fluency.
- The student struggles to effectively use words to express organized and complete thoughts in writing.
- The student's word usage skills are below standard.

Materials Needed

- Markers
- Paper
- Ruler (optional)

Approximate Time Frame for Completion

This lesson plan may take more than one class period, depending on class length.

- Whole group introduction: 5 minutes
- Whole group minilessons: 10 to 15 minutes
- Small group practice: 10 to 15 minutes (variable depending on article length and student participation)
- Independent practice with peer feedback: 10 to 15 minutes

Intervention Procedure and Scripts

Tier One: Whole Group

Explain to students that vocabulary words have a point value determined by the number of syllables in the word. They may use a thesaurus. Each syllable is worth one point. For example, the word *great* is worth 1 point, *immense* is worth 2 points, and *enormous* 3 points. The student groups or teams will earn grades based on the total number of points they receive for their words, as follows:

- 30 points = C
- 40 points = B
- 60 points = A

Tier One: Whole Group

1. Draw a large circle on the board, and write the theme topic in the center of the circle.

2. Have students brainstorm a list of words that come to mind for that theme.

3. One student records the words in the circle on the board.

4. Assign students to pairs. Use the High with Middle, Middle with Low method of choosing pairs (see Figure 2.5 on page 18).

5. Explain to the students that they are going to work with a partner to become an expert on one of the words.

6. Give each student a Vocabulary Word Map (see Figure 3.1 on page 28), and draw one on the board. Choose a word from the board, and complete a vocabulary word map with the class to demonstrate how to complete one properly.

7. Ask one person from each group to share a word map with the class and then post the word map on the board. Students can use them during their writing if they need help with a word.

Tier Two: Small Group (May Also Be Used at Tier One)

1. Put students in groups of two or three, leveled appropriately.

2. Provide each group with a thesaurus and a dictionary.

3. Assign each group one word appropriate to the pair or group's ability level from the lists the class brainstormed.

4. Have students work together to complete their word maps. Each person in the group will complete a word map.

Tier Three: One on One

Students work with a specialist or one on one with the teacher to master the skill.

To Differentiate

- Differentiate by readiness and interest
- Include technology tools such as Inspiration Software, FreeMind, or Compendium

Assessment

Rubric: Creating Vocabulary Word Maps

Category	1	2	3	4
Practice	Makes no attempt to complete the vocabulary word map.	Correctly completes three steps.	Correctly completes four steps.	Correctly completes all five steps: • Writes word in center box. • Records synonyms or a definition. • Records antonyms. • Creates an original sentence using the word. • Draws a picture representing the word.
Gives enough details and/or creativity in sentence	Uses sentences of less than 4 words, lack details or creativity.	Uses an adjective.	Uses an adjective and an adverb.	Uses adjectives, adverbs, and/or metaphors to create memory cue.
Gives enough details in picture	Uses almost no details or creativity.	Gives some details or creativity.	Uses creative imagery and shows thought.	Is very creative and shows thought behind imagery.
Acquisition (vocabulary assessment)	Scores below 70%.	Scores 70% or above.	Scores 80% or above.	Scores 90% or above.

Across the Curriculum

Teachers in social studies, science, and math can use this approach. Students can use vocabulary word maps to learn vocabulary related to new themes and to show connections within themes.

■ SIGNING AS AN INTERVENTION STRATEGY

Research has shown signing vocabulary to be an effective learning tool. It is novel and will be a new concept for almost everyone who reads this book. Consequently, no reader should find this lesson plan boring. Does one have to know American Sign Language (ASL) in order to use this strategy? No. Might the reader have students learn to fingerspell? Yes. This is an option that most intervention specialists never consider using at any level, much less the secondary level. Yet research backs up its significant potential to support reading, literacy, and spelling.

My first experience with using sign language was when I was asked to teach my differentiated instruction strategy seminar at a school for the deaf. I hired a Deaf Education teacher as a consultant to not only attend my seminar and give me critical feedback as to what applied, but also to help me understand the culture and learning methodology of the deaf community. She taught me the seven continents in ASL. We discussed the value of using sign language with hearing children who are also kinesthetic learners. It simply made sense to me and it worked. Yet I had no research to back up use of the strategy in the classroom.

Shortly thereafter, a middle school Language Arts teacher shared with me how she used finger spelling to help students learn their vocabulary words. She found that they not only learned the vocabulary, but spelled the words correctly as well. She and her team were highly enthusiastic about signing vocabulary because it had been such a success.

While researching whether there was data to support the use of sign language and finger spelling, I came across the work of Dr. Philip Prinz and Dr. Marilyn Daniels (Prinz & Strong, 1995, 1997; Daniels, 2001). Dr. Daniels has used sign language with older students. She has a chapter in her book devoted to that demographic.

Research Background

Sign language helps students learn vocabulary and improve their spelling skills. Utilizing sign language in the classroom allows students to process spelling from their orthographic processors and their autonomous memories, creating more internal repetition to help them learn more. Incorporating sign language into a lesson will help students master vocabulary concepts faster, which ultimately improves overall literacy and comprehension (Daniels, 2001).

In a recent study conducted by Dr. Philip M. Prinz, hearing children of deaf parents and hearing children of hearing parents were studied to assess literacy development during early childhood. This study determined that hearing children of deaf parents performed higher and were better early readers than hearing children of hearing parents (Peterson, 2007). Could incorporating a teaching model that utilizes sign language to enhance vocabulary instruction on a particular subject help students internalize more content?

Dr. Marilyn Daniels studies the connection between sign language and literacy. She states, "If sign language constitutes a portion of the reading instruction, the signs actually function as built in pictures for amplifying text" (Daniels, 2001, p. 23). She goes on to explain that "ASL is able to aid children's memory with its autonomous memory store by creating a built in redundancy that establishes two independent language sources for children to use for search and recall" (Daniels, 2001).

In addition to supporting literacy development, using sign language improves spelling. "Studies show that a child's memory of the spelling sequence of words is dramatically improved when he or she is taught spelling with this method [finger spelling]" (Daniels, 2001, p. 22). The reading success of a student relies heavily on spelling ability because learning about spelling

- elaborates and reinforces knowledge in the areas of the brain responsible for text comprehension;

- enhances reading proficiency; and
- allows visual recognition of text to connect with knowledge in the areas of the brain responsible for auditory vocabulary recognition.

    "This brain activity strengthens children's ability not just to induce spellings, but to hear and pronounce words correctly in their oral cavities" (Daniels, 2001, p. 22).

Learning Objectives

- To form a connection between two language stores in the brain to enhance search and recall of vocabulary and word meaning
- To use finger spelling to increase spelling accuracy, which improves auditory processing of auditory language
- To provide students with visual and kinesthetic pictures to enhance reading comprehension

Addresses These Nonresponder Indicators

- The student has difficulty connecting new information with previously learned knowledge.
- The student has difficulty linking prior knowledge with new information.
- The student has language difficulties.
- The student's verbal acquisition is limited.
- The student has the necessary skills but lacks the motivation to complete the academic task (*performance or motivation deficit*).
- The student lacks the necessary skills to perform the academic task (*skill deficit*).
- The student struggles to effectively use words to express organized and complete thoughts in writing.
- The student's word usage skills are below standard.

> Caveat: Teachers do not need to be fluent in sign language to use it with students. Rather, they need to be willing to learn signing along with their students.

Materials Needed

- Copy of vocabulary and spelling words from a relevant unit in your course of study
- Dictionary and thesaurus
- American Sign Language Alphabet Chart (see Figure 3.3 on page 34)
- Pictures that support vocabulary and spelling words
- A source relevant to your course of study: book and movie
- Graphic organizer: Vocabulary Word Map (Figure 3.1)

> The book chosen is to illustrate the concept. You can substitute your own book or use your own vocabulary words as needed.

Approximate Time Frame for Completion

This lesson plan may take more than one class period, depending on class length.

- Whole group strategy (three activities): 30 to 40 minutes
- Small group practice: 10 to 15 minutes (variable, depending on article length and student participation)
- Partner work: 10 to 15 minutes (variable, depending on article length and student understanding)
- Independent practice/peer English language learner, limited English proficiency, etc.: 10 to 15 minutes (variable, depending on student understanding)
- Extension learning: Time is variable

Intervention Procedure and Scripts

Tier One: Whole Group

1. Introduce a book appropriate to your course of study to your students.
    a. Guide a brief discussion about the book genre and potential topic.
    b. Ask students to predict content based on the cover image, title, and back matter copy.

2. Write three vocabulary words from the book on the board. Explain that these are words from the book (example: futile, ideology, nostalgia).

3. Introduce students to the words listed on the board. Read the words aloud with proper enunciation and intonation.

4. Read aloud an excerpt from the book that contains the vocabulary words.
    a. Ask students to use context clues to determine the meaning of the words.
    b. Discuss the potential meaning of each word.
    c. As a class, determine the accurate definition.
    d. Visually demonstrate the word. For example, use the word in a sentence and act it out, or show a picture of the word or the word in action.
    e. Using the Vocabulary Word Map graphic organizer, start demonstrating how to "map" out the word by filling in the word, adding the sentence and definition to the chart, and drawing the picture.

5. Fingerspell the word and/or sign the word with ASL three times, then whisper the definition.

Tier One: Pair Work

1. Explain to the students that they are going to work with a partner until each becomes an expert about the new vocabulary words.

2. Assign students to pairs: Use the High with Middle, Middle with Low method of choosing pairs (see Figure 2.5 on page 18).

3. Give each group the ASL Alphabet Chart (Figure 3.3 on page 34) and five vocabulary words chosen from a relevant source such as the text from your course of study, a list of sight words, or vocabulary critical to successful test taking.

4. Explain to the students that they will take turns stating the word, drawing a picture representing it, and signing the word.

   a. One student will sign the word while his or her partner says or guesses the word.
   b. Repeat this process for each word, with each student taking both roles.

5. Have students complete the Vocabulary Word Map (Figure 3.1) together for each word.

> **Time-saving tip:** If you can gain access to the Gaulladet font and provide students with the five words list typed in both Century Gothic font and Gaulladet font, it will save students from looking up the letters in the chart. This step is not critical; however, it may be helpful depending on your student's ability level.

Figure 3.1   Vocabulary Word Map

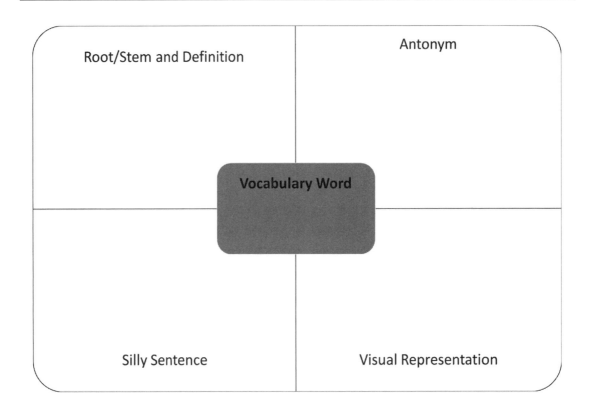

    a. Review how to complete the five sections of the Vocabulary Word Map if necessary. There are many variations of this chart in educational literature and equally varied ways to present it. The specific example shown in this text is one of those variations and not specifically required for this sample lesson plan.

    b. Ensure that students have colored writing utensils to highlight or color-code their map.

6. Once the Vocabulary Word Map is complete, have students find two more words that they do not recognize or know from a relevant text and repeat the above steps using those words.

7. Have one person from each group share one word they found with the class and then post their Vocabulary Word Map for that word on the board so that the students can use it during their writing.

8. After each group has shared its word, randomly review some with the class. For example, if a group picked the word *template*,

    a. practice signing that word and saying as a class; and

    b. follow up by having students quietly fingerspell words as a group.

9. As you become skilled with finger spelling, you will quickly see who is misspelling the word. Collect data on students who are struggling with the process, and adjust interventions based on the data you collect.

Tier Two: Small Group (May Also Be Used at Tier One)

1. Assign students to pairs: Use the High with Middle, Middle with Low method of choosing pairs (see Figure 2.5 on page 18).

2. Each pair will need a thesaurus and a dictionary.

3. Assign each pair one chapter from a book or specific number of pages to read together. (You might assign words appropriate to the pair's or group's ability level.)

4. As students read the chapter aloud, they will underline or write on a separate sheet of paper words that are new to them.

5. When reading is complete, students will work together to complete their vocabulary word maps. Each person in the group will complete a vocabulary word map on at least one new word.

Tier Three: One on One

> **Note:** The following intervention uses ASL. It's perfectly all right to learn along with your students. There are also videos available online to teach ASL. If you are concerned about whether learning ASL is not a good use of time, consider the research on Baby Sign Language in addition to the research results noted above. Learning to sign as a remediation helps students connect the sign language to the meaning of a known word. If the students are below level, it is crucial that they understand the concept of connecting the sign language to the meaning of the word first. If students are struggling to comprehend the meaning of words, they will not make the connection because of their inability to understand the word.

1. Students work with a specialist or one on one with the teacher to master the skill.
2. Start by signing sight words.
3. Introduce a sight word visually in print.
4. Sign and say the word to the student.
5. Student signs with the teacher.
6. Student signs the word without assistance.

To Differentiate

- Differentiate by readiness and interest.
- When showing videos in the classroom, turn on closed captioning. Dr. Philip M. Prinz found that hearing children of deaf parents watch television with closed captioning, which enables them to connect images to words at an early age (Peterson, 2007).
- Use the Gallaudet manual alphabet font: http://simplythebest.net/fonts/fonts/gallaudet.html.

English as a Second Language and English Language Learners

Depending on the student's native language, there may be many English words that have no comparable word in the learner's language. ASL provides a picture for these nonnative words in the student's mind. They make the connection between the sign and the English word (Daniels, 2001).

The purpose for using ASL with English language learner (ELL) students is to provide kinesthetic and visual associations for specific words. I do not recommend this strategy as a tool for teaching syntax.

1. Teach ASL along with English to ELL students to enhance understanding of specific vocabulary words as appropriate.

2. Start by including a physical object that represents that word that you are teaching.

Assessment

Rubric: Creating Vocabulary Word Maps

Category	1	2	3	4
Overall Practice	Makes no attempt to complete the vocabulary word maps or sign the words.	Correctly completes three sections of each of the vocabulary word maps and signs all of the words.	Correctly completes four sections of each of the vocabulary word maps and signs all of the words.	Correctly completes all five sections of each of the vocabulary word maps and signs all of the words.
Writing	Uses fragmented or incomplete sentences.	Uses an adjective in the silly sentences.	Uses an adverb and adjective in the silly sentences.	Uses adjectives, metaphors, and adverbs to generate memory cues.
Picture	Gives no detail or creativity to depict the word.	Gives some detail or creativity to depict the word.	Imagery is creative and shows thought.	Very creative; demonstrates creativity and thought.
Vocabulary and Signing	Recalls fewer than three out of seven of the words learned through sign language.	Recalls at least four out of seven of the words learned through sign language.	Recalls at least five out of seven of the words learned through sign language.	Recalls at least six out of seven of the words learned through sign language.

Across the Curriculum

Teachers in all core subjects can use this approach to help students master concept-specific vocabulary.

- Sign the relationship between historical figures (sibling, parent, child, friend, and so on).
- Incorporate sign language into mnemonic strategies for memorizing critical concepts or basic facts in every subject to internalize content-specific vocabulary.
- Create a rap or song to review instructional material and incorporate signing.
- Show a movie with closed captioning to connect verbal language with visual representation and text for visual learners.
- Teach your curriculum as usual, incorporating sign language at your own pace.

ADDITIONAL VOCABULARY INTERVENTIONS ■

If your school offers ASL as a language, encourage ELL/ESL students and struggling readers to take ASL instead of other foreign languages. This will help these students increase their vocabulary and mastery of the English language, thus improving their overall literacy and comprehension skills.

■ ADDITIONAL NONLINGUISTIC INTERVENTIONS

Many students are bodily-kinesthetic learners. They learn through their bodies and they need to move. They fidget and squirm. The following ideas can help make movement into a positive learning force in your classroom. The first four tips were contributed by Fritz Bell in *Creative Classrooms* (Bell, 2005).

- Have your students act out vocabulary words with their bodies. This will give them a visual picture to remember their words.
- Have the class clap out the syllables in the names of their classmates or their vocabulary words. This is a great strategy for helping kids remember long, multisyllabic words.
- Kinesthetic alphabetizing: Put vocabulary words on individual cards and pass them out to the class. Then have them move around the room and, at a signal from you, form groups of five or less (depending on grade level and vocabulary) and line up in alphabetical order based on the words on their cards.
- Kinesthetic prepositions: Have students use an object such as a pencil and hold it *in, under, over, next to, beside,* or *above* their desks to act out prepositions.
- Have students fingerspell their vocabulary and spelling words (Koehler & Lloyd, 1986). Form pictures to connect to vocabulary for visual vocabulary review cards. Makebeliefscomix.com is a website with wonderful tools for teachers and students alike.
- Building vocabulary skills at home: Suggest to parents that they turn on the closed captioning on TV.

■ COMBINING VERBAL LINGUISTIC AND NONLINGUISTIC INTERVENTIONS: PRACTICE STRATEGIES FOR TIERS ONE, TWO, AND THREE

I'm always looking for ways to make learning motivating and fun. Vocabulary development and spelling are passions of mine that have been building for the past year. I constantly hear teachers lament that students do not remember vocabulary. Reading deficiencies, many times exacerbated by poor vocabulary development, affect test scores, both on state tests and on the SAT and ACT. Students also are developing their own vocabulary and respellings because of text messaging. Those new spellings are making their way into student class work.

So, how about a homework assignment that requires students to create a word collage of sorts? This may require that students have access to a school computer; on a site such as Wordle.net students can access tools that will highlight the most commonly used word in a passage, and thus can visualize vocabulary in an interactive way (Figure 3.2). Wordle.net can also be used by students to check word overuse in a paragraph or essay. The most used words turn out the largest in the design. If the word *nice* is overused, it will be larger than all the other words.

A word of caution: Anyone can upload anything into the Wordle.net gallery. Some students discover very quickly that there are Wordle images that are quite entertaining from a student's standpoint, yet off limits from an educational standpoint. See if it's possible to block the gallery if using this tool in the classroom; otherwise, supervise carefully.

Figure 3.2 Wordle

Figure 3.3 ASL Alphabet Chart

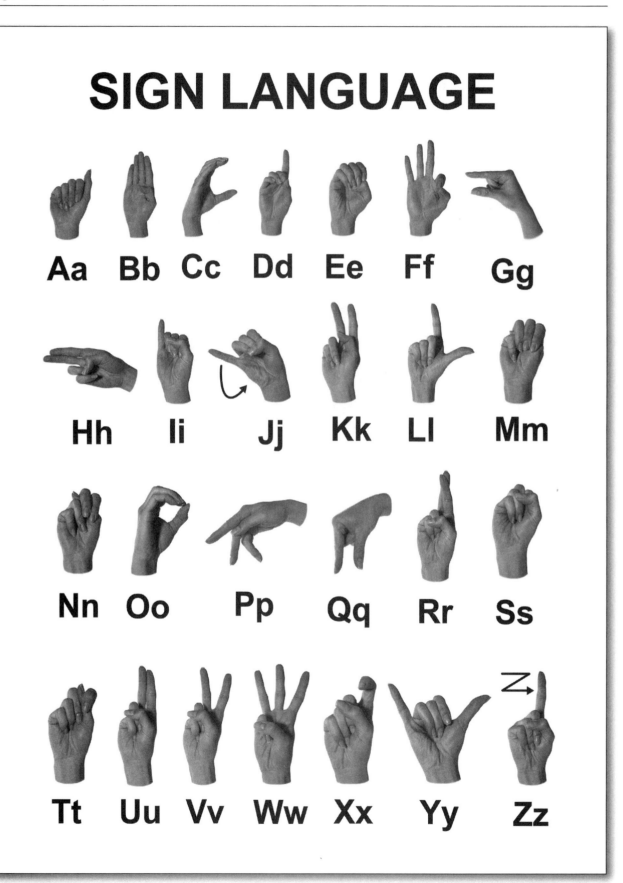

4

Reading Comprehension Intervention Strategies

SOMEBODY-WANTED-BUT-SO ■ SUMMARY STRATEGY

The Somebody-Wanted-But-So strategy (SWBS) demonstrated in this lesson can be used during or after a reading to help students understand literary elements such as conflicts and resolutions. It can also be used as a summation tool in social studies and other subjects. Students complete the strategy on a chart by identifying who (*Somebody*) wanted something (their goal or motivation, what they *Wanted*), what conflict (*But*) arose from the character's desire, and the resolution (*So*) of the conflict. The strategy is outlined step by step in the following lesson.

I chose fairy tales, cultural fables, and legends for this sample lesson because of their familiarity to students. Most youth can relate to these stories and connect the issues, conflicts, and personalities presented in them to their personal lives. These connections support reading comprehension and enhance long-term recall.

In addition, the brevity of this genre allows for repetition and frequency, which is ideal for initial instruction as well as an intervention. Time constraints pose significant challenges to the secondary teacher, especially at the high school level. Utilizing short texts supports the learning objective without requiring significant class time.

Research Background

Reading comprehension is a complex intellectual process that involves two main abilities: understanding word meanings and reasoning with verbal concepts. Without these abilities, students cannot comprehend and in turn do not internalize what they read. Comprehension happens within a reader's mind, which means it cannot be measured in a tangible fashion. Comprehension can only be measured by inferring from a reader's overt behavior (Opitz, Rubin, & Erekson, 2011). The use of strategies helps teachers infer how well a student comprehends the material read. Summarizing, recall, and inferential reading are all methods of determining a student's comprehension of text (Gunning, 2008).

To comprehend expository text, students must discern main ideas and concepts in the text, whereas with literary texts students must identify key elements to summarize a story completely. Summarizing materials allows students to connect to material in a personal manner, as they have the opportunity to make a connection from personal experience to the text (Gunning, 2008). Summarizing allows students to synthesize, analyze, and evaluate material, which develops higher-order thinking skills. However, most students lack the ability to write a summary in a concise manner. When summarizing, students need to identify what happened in the story and state the main details. Most students tend to rewrite the story and tell the teacher everything that happened to demonstrate that they read the passage. This is not a summary. A summary will summarize what the story was about in a concise and explicit manner. Using graphic organizers and the SWBS strategy encourages students to develop concise summaries of literature.

Learning Objectives

- To develop higher-order comprehension strategies to understand and interpret literature
- To use literature to master the SWBS strategy to summarize material concisely
- To provide students with the skills and ability to connect with text beyond basic literal comprehension
- To expand and increase vocabulary

Addresses These Nonresponder Indicators

- The student has difficulty connecting new information with previously learned knowledge.
- The student has difficulty organizing information.
- The student has language difficulties.
- The student's verbal acquisition is limited.
- The student has low clerical aptitude or difficulty completing written work.
- The student's notetaking skills are deficient.
- The student has difficulty effectively using words to express organized and complete thoughts in writing.
- The student's word usage skills are below standard.

Materials Needed

- Three to five short stories such as fairy tales (for example, *Cinderella*), cultural fables, and legends
- Summary Graphic Organizer (see Figure 4.2 on page 71)
- SWBS handout (see Figure 4.3 on page 72)
- Paper and pencils
- Movie version of the short story (if applicable)
- Short cartoon of your choice (many are available on the Internet for free and instantly)

> If the Internet or a DVD player is not available to show a short cartoon of your choice, substitute a picture book that appeals to adolescents.

Approximate Time Frame for Completion

This lesson plan may take more than one class period, depending on class length.

- Whole group minilessons: 15 minutes each.
- Partner work brainstorms: 5 minutes (variable, depending on article length and student understanding).
- Partner work or small group practice: 10 to 15 minutes (variable, depending on article length and student participation).
- Independent practice with peer feedback: 10 to 15 minutes (variable, depending on article length and student understanding).
- Extension learning: Time is variable. Novels and lengthy stories can be taught over the course of days and weeks.

Intervention Procedure and Scripts

Tier One: Partner Work

1. Assign students to pairs using the High with Middle, Middle with Low grouping strategy (see Figure 2.5 on page 18). Give each pair one sheet of paper.

2. Write the title *What We Know About Summaries* on the paper.

3. Give students five minutes to brainstorm anything they can remember about summaries.

4. Make it a contest: How much can they list on the paper? Which pair can come up with the most items?

Tier One: Whole Class

1. Whip around the room, allowing each pair to list one thing they know about summaries. If necessary, go around the room a second time to include more feedback.

2. Make a bulleted list on the board of student responses and determine an appropriate class definition of *summary*.

3. Explain to the class why summaries are important and why summarizing is a necessary skill for comprehension.

4. Write *Cinderella*, or the title of another familiar short tale that you believe is grade-level appropriate, on the board. It is important to teach this strategy with a known story for students to conceptualize how the strategy works.

5. Ask them what the story is about, their favorite parts, how it differs from the movie if there was one, and similar questions.

6. Read the story aloud.

7. Explain to the class that when they summarize a piece of literature they must identify
   o the main character;
   o the goal of the main character;
   o the problem or conflict in the story; and
   o the resolution.

8. Everything other than the preceding four points is supplementary to an efficient summary; however, those details are always required in a summarization.

Tier One: Partner Work

1. Have students return to their pairs.

2. Provide each pair with one sheet of paper.

3. Write the title *Details We Remember From the Story* on the paper.

4. Give students five minutes to brainstorm anything they can remember.

5. Make it a contest: How much can they list on the paper?

Tier One: Whole Class

1. Whip around the room, allowing each pair to list one thing they know about the story. If necessary, go around the room a second time to include more feedback.

2. Make a list on the board of everything the students volunteer.

3. Explain that this list is not concise and does not explicitly tell the reader what happened in the story.

4. Explain that as they read they need to be able to determine if something is fact or an opinion instead of looking at the information for what it literally means. Select a fact from the list as an example and tell the students that when they read this fact, they know exactly what happened. When someone is expressing his or her feeling or perspective about something, it's an opinion.

5. Make four columns on the board. Label the columns with *Somebody, Wanted, But,* and *So* at the top. See the following example.

6. Complete the columns as a class. Explain that if there is more than one main character or a more complex plot, then they can add rows to the columns.

Somebody	Wanted	But	So
Anne Frank	to hide from the Nazis	someone turned her in	she died in a concentration camp
Annie Sullivan	to help Helen Keller learn to communicate and learn	Helen was unable to speak, see, or hear and was very willful	Annie convinced Helen's parents to allow her to take Helen to a house separate from the rest of the family so that Helen had to depend on Annie

Tier One/Tier Two: Small Group

1. Assign students to groups of four: Use the High with Middle, Middle with Low grouping strategy (see Figure 2.5 on page 18).

2. Give students three different short stories—one popular story and two lesser-known stories. Your class literature text should provide ample choices.

3. Pass out three copies each of the Summary Graphic Organizer (Figure 4.2 on page 71) and SWBS Table Graphic Organizer (Figure4.3 on page 72).

4. Give each student in each group of four a different color marker, pencil, or crayon.

5. Have students put their names on the paper in their color.

6. Tell students they can choose which story to read as a group. Students may choose one person in the group to read aloud; however, they must read in quiet voices so as not to disturb other groups. They may also take turns reading aloud.

7. Instruct students to complete the Summary Graphic Organizer after they read their selection, taking turns filling in the chart with their color.

    a. *Important:* Students take turns listing their words in the chart by passing the paper around the table. They list their words and phrases in their different colors.

    b. Tell students that you expect to see all four colors on the paper.

8. Instruct students to complete both the SWBS Table Graphic Organizer and the Summary Graphic Organizer using their knowledge of what happened in the story.

9. Once students have completed the charts, have the students write a one-paragraph summary as a group, using the points recorded in the Summary Graphic Organizer and the SWBS Table Graphic Organizer to make the summary concise and to the point.

> *Note to high school teachers:* I used to be reluctant to use crayons with Grades 9 through 12 until I was faced with a tight budget. Crayons work just fine and can be a lesson in frugality for students. Simply state the realities of your budget. If they want to bring in their own markers, they can. Otherwise, if all you can afford is crayons, they work just fine.

Tier One: Whole Group

1. Ask one person from each group to share the group's summary with the class.

2. After each group has shared its summary, choose one story to discuss. (*Tip:* Pick a story that is not well known to the students to see if the class has a good idea of what happened from one of the group's summaries.)

3. Reinforcement activity: If available, play a short video cartoon or read a picture book (sophisticated or with an adult theme) to your students. Encourage them to take notes on their SWBS Graphic Organizers to help remember key points.

4. When you are finished reading the story or watching the cartoon, randomly prompt students to think about a part of the story or cartoon and identify what part of the SWBS formula it is. For example, if you state the main character's name, then the students should say that it is *Somebody*.

Tier Two/Small Group (May Also Be Used at Tier One)

1. Assign students to small groups of four students. Use the High with Middle, Middle with Low method of choosing groups (see Figure 2.5 on page 18).

2. Each group will need a chapter book (see note) to read and the handouts for the SWBS Table Graphic Organizer (Figure 4.3 on page 72) and Beginning, Middle and End Graphic Organizer (Figure 4.4 on page 73).

> *Note:* Again, we are using chapter books with mature themes because they are an ideal length and reading level for practicing this skill. If you prefer to substitute another resource that you believe is more appropriate at the secondary level, do so. Be careful, however, to select a piece of the appropriate reading level and length.

3. Explain to students that they will read a chapter you assign them from the book.

4. When they have finished reading the assigned chapter, have students complete the SWBS Table Graphic Organizer together. The students are to summarize only the assigned chapter. This helps them identify and learn how to apply summarization techniques in more complex and difficult storylines.

5. Complete the storyboard on the Beginning, Middle, and End Graphic Organizer to conceptualize the summary and story visually.

6. Have students share their summary with another group.

7. Monitor their progress by walking around the room and listening for mastery to assess their understanding of the concept.

   a. Collect data by targeting specific students and asking essential questions. Document their responses.

   b. Coach and correct as needed to ensure that the students internalize material.

Tier Three: One on One

1. Students work with a specialist or one on one with the teacher to master the skill.

2. Have the students read a simple picture book or well-known short story.

3. The student and specialist should read the story together.

4. Have them discuss what the story is about together.

5. Then have them complete the SWBS Table Graphic Organizer (Figure 4.3 on page 72) together step by step. Thoroughly explain each step.

6. Provide correction and explanation as needed.

7. Practice with at least two stories.

To Differentiate

- Work at the developmental and reading level of students.
- Instead of writing, let students draw pictures to identify the Somebody-Wanted-But-So.
- Show an excerpt from movies about the same topic and then complete the summary.
- Have students act out the summary and each part of the concept.

Assessment

Rubric: All Handouts

Category	1	2	3	4
Overall Practice	Makes no attempt to complete the handout or summarize the story according to the concept.	Attempts to complete the handout and makes minimal effort within the group.	Completes the handout and makes efforts to summarize the story according to the concept. Participates in the group discussion.	Correctly completes the handouts and 1. Summarizes the story according to the concept 2. Identifies the characters, setting, and problem through the concept 3. Demonstrates proficiency in the assignment 4. Contributes actively to the discussions and class work as a whole
Writing	Uses sentence fragments or does not complete.	Provides minimal explanation and use of sentences on assignment.	Clearly explains the summary in a concise manner. Writes proficient and complete sentences.	Clearly and concisely explains the summary in a superior fashion. Writes proficient and complete sentences that are free from grammatical and syntax errors.
Critical Reading Applications	Identifies the SWBS less than 60% of the time when prompted.	Identifies the SWBS at least 60% of the time when prompted.	Identifies the SWBS at least 70% of the time when prompted.	Identifies the SWBS at least 80% of the time when prompted.

Across the Curriculum

Social studies, science, and math teachers can use this approach to have their students master concept-specific vocabulary.

- Have students summarize passages and events that are relevant to the subject matter taught. For example, summarize what happened at a battle in the Civil War or how a scientist invented something.
- Have students read a story that incorporates math equations. Have them summarize the story and complete the problems.
- Show an excerpt from a movie derived from the book or story you read.

Vocabulary Interventions

1. With English language learner (ELL) students, have them read a story that is from their native culture and complete the summarization within a context they already understand.

2. Then have them practice within American culture and English to make the connection.

READING COMPREHENSION ■
INTERVENTION: RECIPROCAL TEACHING

After the first semester of my son's freshman year in college, he told me that many of the students in the dorm with him did not even attend classes. He said, "Mom, at least I go to class! Sometimes I have trouble staying awake during those long lectures, but I'm there." I responded, "Ian, do you fall asleep in class? How can you learn if you are falling asleep?" He gave me that look that only a teen seems to perfect that said, "What are you thinking?" He reminded me, "Mom, you *know* that I don't learn from the teacher talking. I go to class so I look good. Then, I learn it from the teaching assistant (TA) or with my friends."

Research studies abound to validate that peer learning is a powerful teaching tool for the majority of students. To not utilize peer learning, whether you call it cooperative learning, reciprocal teaching, peer tutoring, or *Think-Pair-Share*, is to put many students at a disadvantage. This is especially true when engaging nonlinguistic learners or students with limited English proficiency (LEP).

Reciprocal teaching and cooperative learning are important for LEP students, because they typically speak their native language at home and in the community. They speak their native language in the hall and in the cafeteria because they usually gravitate towards friendships with students who speak their language. If they are silent in class because the class is teacher-directed, they have almost no opportunity during the school day to speak English. My experience as a teacher coach in schools with high LEP populations confirms that this is the case.

Research Background

Reciprocal teaching (Lederer, 2000) is an instructional strategy involving discussion as well as the use of reading strategies (summarizing, question generating, clarifying, and predicting) to improve comprehension of text. Studies by Palinscar and Brown (O'Donnell & King, 1999) indicated that reciprocal teaching greatly influences student comprehension skills. When participating in reciprocal teaching, students became more independent readers and better summarizers, predictors, and critical thinkers. As an additional benefit, they found that students who participated in reciprocal teaching groups also displayed fewer behavior problems. "Reciprocal teaching, when used consistently, can produce rapid results and growth in comprehension for readers of all ages" (Oczkus, 2003, p. 26).

This lesson plan focuses on using reciprocal teaching in the form of discussion, role-playing, and Think-Pair-Share to practice a questioning strategy. According to Shira Lubliner, students "automatically increase their reading comprehension when they read the text, process the meaning, make inferences and connections to prior knowledge, and finally, generate a question" (Oczkus, 2003, p. 15).

Learning Objectives

- To identify the different types of questions that can be asked to improve reading comprehension
- To formulate different types of questions to enhance understanding and recall

- To gain experience with cooperative groups to practice reading comprehension strategies
- To synthesize information in order to respond to a variety of questions
- To interpret text and demonstrate higher-level thinking skills in creating various types of questions
- To apply questioning strategies to content area texts

Addresses These Nonresponder Indicators

- The accuracy and pace of the student's performance require extensive effort in order to support reading.
  - The student has Attention Deficit Disorder.
  - There is a breakdown in the student's ability to process information in a way that is personally meaningful.
- The student has difficulty determining what is important in a text.
  - The student has difficulty linking prior knowledge to new information.
  - The student has difficulty retaining information.
  - There have been gaps in the prior instruction the student has received.
  - The student is gifted, but becomes bored easily, has problems remaining engaged, or suffers from a lack of motivation.
  - The student has problems finding textual support.
- The student has reading difficulties.
- The student has problems with reading fluency.
- The student's self-questioning techniques are nonexistent or not developed enough to support understanding while reading.
  - The student has trouble organizing information.

Materials Needed

- Literature (magazine or newspaper articles, textbooks, poetry, novels, short stories, non-fiction and fiction texts, websites, blogs)
- Questioning Web handout (see Figure 4.5 on page 74)

Approximate Time Frame for Completion

This lesson plan may take more than one class period, depending on class length.

- Whole group strategy (three activities): 30 to 40 minutes
- Small group practice: 10 to 15 minutes (variable, depending on article length and student participation)
- Partner work: 10 to 15 minutes (variable, depending on article length and student understanding)
- Independent practice with peer feedback: 10 to 15 minutes (variable, depending on article length and student understanding)

Intervention Procedure and Scripts

Tier One: Whole Group

The key to teaching students how to use a particular reading strategy is modeling that strategy. Through Think-Alouds, teachers can demonstrate how to ask questions throughout a reading (James & Carter, 2007). When Think-Alouds are combined with the Question Answer Relationship (QAR) strategy (Raphael, Highfield, & Au, 2006), students are maximizing two tools to support reading comprehension. Both these tools can be used as an intervention strategy.

Explain to students that there are two kinds of questions in the QAR strategy: those in the book and those in their heads.

1. Questions in the Book
   a. "Right There" questions are clearly answered in the text. (You might call the "Right There" questions Green Light questions because students can "go" right to the text for the answers.)
   b. "Think and Search" questions are answered within the text, but the reader has to search for the answer and synthesize material to find it. (You might call these questions Yellow Light questions because the reader must "slow down and proceed with caution!")

2. Questions in the Reader's Head
   a. "On My Own" questions can be answered by the reader by synthesizing prior knowledge. (You might call these questions Red Light questions because the reader must "Stop!" and think about the response.)
   b. "Author and Me" questions are those in which the answer can be inferred from the text. The reader must use a combination of textual information and prior knowledge to answer the question. These are also Red Light questions.

3. Choose a book or article for modeling the questioning strategy.

4. To ensure maximum participation, give each student three colored cards (one green, one red, and one yellow), corresponding to the three types of questions.

5. Read the selection aloud to the students.

6. Model the thinking behind the QAR strategy by asking questions related to the text.
   a. "I wonder why the author included this"
   b. "What is a _____?"
   c. "How would I feel if this happened to me?"

7. Tell students to hold up the colored card that matches the type of question that you ask.

8. Randomly question student thinking. "Why did you choose a yellow card for this question?"

9. Sum up the whole class lesson with a visual representation of the concept. In doing so, you will solidify the concepts for visual learners as well as engage other parts of the brain in storing information in long-term memory.

10. Create a Questioning Web (Figure 4.5 on page 74) on chart paper.

11. Go over the Questioning Web and discuss what type of QAR question each one exemplifies.

Tier One/Tier Two: Small Group

Role-play: Interviewing for QARs

1. Assign students to small groups of four students. Use the High with Middle, Middle with Low grouping strategy (see Figure 2.5 on page 18).

2. Choose a short piece of text for students to read. Consider text that is short, easy to read, and contains an age appropriate theme (short articles, picture books, chapter books, nonfiction material at a variety of reading levels).

3. Either read the text aloud to the students or have students read in their groups.

4. After reading specified material:
   a. Choose one student in each group to be the interviewee.
   b. Pull the interviewees aside to prep them for their role. Explain to the interviewees that they will take on the role of a character in the reading. They will play the role of a historical figure, a scientist, or whatever fits the chosen text for this activity. The rest of the class will be the interviewers. Interviewees should try to "be their character" and use information from the reading to guide their responses.

5. While you are prepping the interviewees, the other students should work in their groups to formulate questions.
   a. Each student interviewer must come up with at least two questions to ask the interviewee. They may collaborate with the other interviewers in their small group to support different ability levels and ensure there is no duplication of questions.
   b. Challenge interviewers to be sure that their group will ask one question from each QAR category.
   c. Explain to interviewers that they will take turns asking questions and eliciting responses from the interviewees.

6. After interviewees have been prepped and the interviewers have completed their questions, have interviewees rejoin their groups and begin the activity.

7. Walk around the room and collect data, take notes, and encourage and support students as they engage in the activity.

8. Wrap up the discussion. Have students give examples of questions from each QAR category that were asked by classmates.

Tier One/Tier Two: Partner Work

Role-play: Teacher and Student

In this intervention activity, students will practice being the "teacher" and the "student." The "teacher" will ask the "student" questions. This strategy not only emphasizes questioning ("teacher"), but also reinforces other comprehension strategies ("student" and "teacher") such as summarizing, and synthesizing, depending on the types of questions the "teacher" creates.

1. Assign students partners. Use the High with Middle, Middle with Low grouping strategy (see Figure 2.5 on page 18). Appoint one student in each pair the role of "teacher" and the other the role of "student."

2. Provide each pair with reading material (pages in a textbook, a literature chapter, an article, etc.) and have them read the material together.

3. Have each pair fill out a Questioning Web (Figure 4.5 on page 74) while they are reading. Suggest that they stop after each half page or each full page and write down the information from that section rather than wait until they have read the entire piece. Students might benefit from drawing stick figure symbols to represent key words, ideas, and questions.

4. When students have completed their webs, the "teacher" asks the "student" questions, using the Questioning Web as a guide. The "student" responds to the questions using the text for support.

5. When they are finished, they can switch roles. Challenge the "student" to think of additional questions the "teacher" did not ask.

6. When role-play is complete and both students in the pair have had their turn, instruct students to evaluate each question according to the QAR guidelines. Encourage them to tally how many times they used each type of QAR question. If they had trouble creating certain types of questions, they can work together to create new questions to fill in the gap.

Tier Three: Specialist/Teacher and Student

Instead of the teacher-student role-play outlined above, implement the strategy with a student paired with a classroom teacher, specialist, or paraprofessional skilled in the QAR method.

Alternate Grouping Suggestions

- Random grouping (counting off, toe-to-toe, etc.)
- Strong reader with struggling reader
- Similar ability levels (adjust material accordingly)
- Use the High with Middle, Middle with Low grouping strategy (see Figure 2.5 on page 18)

To Differentiate

- Bookmark Cue Card: Provide students with a QAR Bookmark (see Figure 4.6 on page 75) or a desk template to help them remember the different types of questions.
- Brainstorm to Sort:
  - Have students use a Questioning Web to brainstorm questions from a text or math problem.
  - Sort the questions according to the QAR model. This frees up the students' working memories to create questions without the added step of categorizing. Categorize according to QAR later.

- Same Ability QAR: Students can work in groups to create questions. Assign students who are experiencing the most difficulty formulating questions the "Right There" questions and the most advanced students the "Author and Me" questions.

Application Example

Your class just finished reading the first chapter of *The Story of My Life* by Helen Keller.

1. Assign each student a partner.

2. Each pair develops a Questioning Web (Figure 4.5 on page 74) together.

3. Students work together to classify each question into one of the QAR categories.

4. Choose four students to be the interviewees. They will represent Helen's mother, Helen's brother, Helen's father, and Helen.

5. The rest of the class will take turns addressing questions to each character.

6. Make a giant chart and have the class give examples of each type of question asked.

7. Discuss what types of questions students find easier and harder to compose and answer. Have students offer suggestions to classmates on how to overcome obstacles.

Across the Curriculum

This strategy can be applied to many curricular areas. For example:

- *Social Studies and Science*: Have students use the QAR strategy to guide questions for a research project.
- *Tests:* Use the QAR strategy to help students study for a test in any course.
- *Math:* The QAR framework supports comprehension of word problems, especially in relation to graphs or tables displaying data.

For Independent Writing Assignments

Use the QAR questions to support independent writing assignments such as research projects, journaling, or essay writing.

For Independent Reading Assignments
(Literature or Content Area)

Use the questioning strategy as a tool to check for understanding.

For Group Brainstorming and Mind Map Creation

The questioning strategy is ideal for cooperative learning. Students can challenge one another, help one another understand material, and develop discussions through questioning.

Extension

Students may select their own articles in order to find material that meets their interests and academic ability level. They can create quizzes for one another and pose questions that lead to further research and investigation.

QAR Authentic Assessment Activity

- Have students practice the QAR approach independently.
- Read a piece of literature and write down their questions using a Questioning Web as they read.
- Have them use the QAR Graphic Organizer (see Figure 4.7 on page 76) to categorize each of their questions.
- Go back and add more questions to any categories that need more. Students should try to answer their own questions.
- Exchange papers with a partner. Answer the questions and provide feedback on the quality of questions.

Assessment

Rubric: Summarizing Pieces of Literature

Category	1	2	3	4
In the Book: "Right There" Questions and "Think and Search" Questions	Does not identify or create "In the Book" questions accurately.	Does not consistently identify or create "In the Book" questions.	Accurately identifies and creates "In the Book" questions.	Identifies and creates "In the Book" questions appropriately linked to the text, reflecting close, careful reading.
In My Head: "On My Own" Questions and "Author and Me" Questions	Does not identify or create "In My Head" questions accurately.	Does not consistently identify or create "In My Head" questions.	Accurately identifies and creates "In My Head" questions.	Identifies and creates "In My Head" questions with clarity of thought and higher-level thinking skills (demonstrates perceptive reading skills).

PICTURE BOOKS: A SECONDARY ■ READING INTERVENTION

Many years ago, when I was co-teaching science, I found the reading level of the textbooks far above the reading level of many students in the classroom. In order to provide materials that covered the content being presented at a reading level that supported all students, I worked with our high school librarian to obtain nonfiction books at a variety of reading levels that were related to the unit we were studying.

For example, when we were studying the solar system, I was able to obtain picture books on that topic, as well as books at the college level. I'd make these books available to students in the classroom for use as supplemental reading or background material for projects. I was always amazed at who picked up which books. At times, honors students chose a picture book to read and students with special needs chose a college-level text. The students seemed to use a variety of the books regardless of their reading level.

Consequently, I've always been a believer in providing books at all reading levels, including picture books as supplemental reading for secondary students. When considering both novel and staid examples for lesson plans in this book, the picture book seemed to be an obvious choice. While at first thought picture books may seem too elementary for high school students, it's amazing how many students—after they make their wisecracks—actually dig in and enjoy working with the picture books; they are an "easy" focus. Furthermore, starting with simple and easy books facilitates the acquisition of the standards-based skills. The research I've cited below backs up the benefits of using picture books at the high school level as well as with ELL students in the secondary classroom.

Research Background

Picture books used in the upper grade levels may improve student comprehension. In a study by Bridget Robinson at the University of North Carolina (Robinson, 2007), high school students who studied literary terms with picture books were 72% more successful on a test of literary terms than those who studied using traditional means. Students found it easier to understand and recall literary terms when picture books were used as a teaching tool.

Picture books help students create mental models (Bickmore, 2001) and help readers build schema. They are written at a reading level accessible to most readers, with content varying to meet individual needs. They help students understand complex ideas and vocabulary. Consider that although picture books typically are written for pre-K children, they are meant to be read aloud and therefore utilize high-level vocabulary. We are also finding more and more picture books with adult themes.

The shorter length of picture books permits students to practice their reading strategies and enhance their understanding of difficult content (Fox & Short, 2003). Picture books allow teachers to "bring up issues, problems, and concerns without deluging students with facts and information" (Harvey & Goudvis, 2007, p. 69). Another advantage to the shorter length of picture books is that student reading and response is plausible within the brief class periods educators face in secondary schools (Johnson & Giorgis, 2007).

For the ELL student, picture books provide a nonthreatening tool with visual cues to support English-language acquisition. In a research study focused on using picture books and literature-based instruction with high school ESL students, Nancy L. Hadaway and JaNae Mundy found that using picture books engaged students in the language learning process. Vocabulary increased, and reading comprehension skills were evident through class discussion and through writing about their reading experience through journaling, poetry, and research presentations (Hadaway & Mundy, 1999).

Learning Objectives

- To use picture books to improve comprehension
- To identify factual text within picture books
- To make connections to their personal lives, other texts, and the world
- To synthesize information and present it in a way that is meaningful to students
- To use coding as a reading comprehension and recall strategy

Addresses These Nonresponder Indicators

- The accuracy and pace of the student's reading performance requires extensive effort in order to support reading.
- The student has Attention Deficit Disorder.
- The student has difficulty finding and noting text support for future reference and recall.
- The student has difficulty connecting new information with previously learned knowledge.
- The student has problems determining what is important in a text.
- The student has processing disorders.
- The student's reading difficulties create gaps in understanding.
- The student's reading fluency is not at grade level.
- The student's self-questioning techniques are nonexistent or not developed enough to support understanding while reading.

Materials Needed

- Picture books related to the topic being discussed

Useful Websites

- Picture books for secondary students: http://www.uiowa.edu/~crl/bibliographies/pdf/picbooks_print.pdf.
- Picture books for older readers: http://picturebooksforolderreaders .pbworks.com/.

Approximate Time Frame for Completion

- Whole group: 30 minutes (variable, depending on discussion)
- Small group: 20 minutes (variable, depending on book length and student participation)
- Independent practice: 30 minutes (variable, depending on book length and student understanding)

Intervention Procedure and Scripts

Tier One: Whole Group

First-Level Strategy: Picture Books

Use picture books as a springboard for a new unit of study. They will capture the students' interest, provide visual images and background information, and, if you choose a high quality book with a mature theme, trigger questions and discussions that you can use to guide further instruction.

1. Choose a picture book that meets your instructional purpose.
2. Read the story aloud to the class. Make sure all students can see the powerful pictures. A document camera is helpful though not required.
3. Discuss the book. Some guiding questions might be
   a. What did you learn about the subject from this story?
   b. What questions do you have about this topic?
   c. What would you like to know more about?
   d. What emotions did this story create inside of you?
   e. What facts did this story provide?
   f. What impact did the illustrations have in the story?
   g. What are the benefits of using picture books to understand this concept (if your students are skeptical about using picture books)?
   h. How did (the specific situation) impact (the specific character)? How can you relate?
4. Wrap up by tying the key concepts pulled from the book to the current instructional unit.

Tier One/Tier Two: Small Group

Take It Up a Level: Coding Strategy as an Intervention

The *coding strategy* (Harvey & Goudvis, 2007) is a great way to help students practice finding the important information in texts. Use fictional picture books to teach a particular concept. Take this strategy up a level by teaching students to code the text. By coding the text, they will be able to sort out the relevant information from unnecessary information. They will also incorporate reading comprehension strategies while thinking critically about the text. Students should use sticky notes to code their information and can use any code that makes sense to them. Some suggested codes are

- (L) Learned New Fact
- (*) Interesting Information
- (E) Evoked Emotion
- (?) Questions
- (T) Thoughts
- (C) Connections

1. Assign students to small groups of four students: Use the High with Middle, Middle with Low grouping strategy (see Figure 2.5 on page 18).

2. Give each group a picture book related to your learning goal.

3. Instruct each group member to read one page at a time aloud, using quiet voices.

4. Tell students that after each page, they should discuss any passages they found in the text for which a code would be useful.

5. On each sticky note, students should write the letter code that applies to the specific information, and write a few words to remind them of their thinking.

6. Some students may benefit by adding illustrations to their sticky notes.

7. Repeat this process through the entire book, handout, article, or essay.

8. Explain that when students are finished, they are to review all of their notes.

Tier Three: One on One

Both picture book reading and the coding strategy are intensive intervention options. The picture book strategy is an intervention that could eventually be eliminated with skill mastery. The coding strategy is a learning tool that students could use throughout high school and college.

Optional Activities

- *Fact Blast:* Students list all of the facts they learned through reading the text. If all students are reading the same text, do a whip-around so that students can share the facts they have identified.
- Once students have coded questions on sticky notes and placed them in the text, have them research answers to their questions.
- *Emotional Reaction:* Write a reaction to one of the parts that evoked emotion or thought.
- *Personal Connection:* Discuss connections to other texts, self, and world.

To Differentiate

Using picture books allows for a multitude of options for differentiation.

- Use picture books with no text, and have students provide information based on the pictures.
- Vary the use of nonfiction and fiction picture books.
- Challenge students to find primary sources on a topic. The Internet makes it easier to locate primary sources now than at any other time in history. Students are no longer limited by print and microfilm. Historical documents, letters, maps, and photos of ancient artifacts are often available online.
- Make assignments as focused or broad as the individual student requires.

Application Example

Use picture books to support and increase understanding of a thematic unit. For example, you may be doing a unit on "Tough Times." Each student can choose a different picture book that pertains to this topic. This is such a general topic that students may interpret it as war, poverty, death, or some other theme.

1. Each student chooses a book related to the theme. Examples include
   o *Rose Blanc* by Roberto Innocenti (World War II);
   o *Aunt Harriet's Underground Railroad in the Sky* by Jeanette Winter (slavery);
   o *Fly Away Home* by Eve Bunting (homelessness); and
   o *My Hiroshima* by Junko Morimoto (Hiroshima bombing).

2. Students read their books and complete a graphic organizer that highlights the story line, or a QAR graphic organizer, a Venn diagram, or some other graphic device.

3. Hold class discussions or assign writing prompts in which all students relate their book to the overall theme.

4. What situations in your own life can you relate to the situation in your book?

5. How does your book demonstrate "Tough Times"?

6. What lessons did you learn in your book that you can apply to any tough times you may face in your life?

7. What events and details in the story made it seem real to you? What feelings did those events evoke?

Across the Curriculum

This strategy can be applied to many curricular areas.
In English, use picture books to teach literary devices. Here are some ideas:

- alliteration (*Chicken Little* by Steven Kellogg)
- metaphor (*The Stranger* by Chris Van Allsburg)
- irony (*The Frog Prince, Continued* by Jon Scieszka)
- satire (*The Happy Hocky Family* by Lane Smith)
- personification (*Sylvester and the Magic Pebble* by William Steig)
- symbolism (*Tar Beach* by Faith Ringgold)

In social studies, use picture books to help students relate to a character, time period, and situation.

- Civil War (*Nettie's Trip South* by Ann Turner)
- Holocaust (*The Butterfly* by Patricia Polacco)
- World War II (*All Those Secrets of the World* By Jane Yolen)

In science, use picture books to help students understand complex scientific principles. Students might create their own illustrations to exemplify a concept or to explain a concept in simplified terms, as if teaching it to a young child (*Science Verse* by Jon Scieszka).

In math, have students create picture books to break down the steps of solving a higher-level mathematical problem. Many great picture books teach mathematical concepts, such as the *Sir Cumference* series by Cindy Neuschwander.

Use picture books to model writing traits (Spandel & Culham, 1994).

For Independent Writing Assignments

Picture books are excellent resources to guide writing. They teach grammar rules, sentence structure, sentence fluency, word choice, syntax, writing for specific purposes, organization, and creativity. Students can find examples within picture books or create their own books.

For Independent Reading Assignments
(Literature or Content Area)

Students can apply the coding strategy and the comprehension skills it develops to more sophisticated types of literature including novels, textbooks, websites, and poetry.

For Group Brainstorming and Mind Map Creation

Students can help one another to understand a process or idea through brainstorming and mind mapping. They can work together to locate, read, or create picture books.

Extension

The use of picture books lends itself to a myriad of extension activities. The lesson ideas above list many suggestions. One key to motivating students is to provide choice. For example, they could choose a particular theme and create a bibliography of children's books that pertain to that idea.

- Read a picture book and use sticky notes to code information.
- Have students practice coding picture books independently.
- Have students find 10 different picture books on a specific topic and complete a graphic organizer (see Figure 4.8 on page 77) for each book. They will choose the best book to present to the class.
- Have students write their own children's book, either fiction or nonfiction, about a specific topic.
- Complete a Venn diagram comparing and contrasting a picture book with a textbook (or compare and contrast two picture books on the same topic).
- Use picture books to frame a research project.

Assessment

Rubric: Coding Text to Enhance Comprehension Skills

Category	1	2	3	4
Facts	Is unable to pull the facts from text.	Locates some facts but confuses some facts from the text with nonfactual information.	Locates most of the factual information in a variety of texts.	Locates concrete and inferential facts in a variety of texts.
Questions	Does not formulate questions from the text.	Asks very literal questions from the text.	Asks many different types of questions.	Shows keen comprehension of the text with general questions relating to the "big picture," inferential questions; often researches for more information.
Connections	Does not relate text to other examples.	Makes loose or limited (text, self, world only) connections.	Makes valid connections.	Connects with other text, self, and the world; relates specific situations to big picture ideas.

■ FIGURATIVE LANGUAGE

It seems that one of the most significant reading challenges for students at the secondary level, especially ELL students, is figurative language. Idioms, in particular, are exceptionally problematic. Although I'm not trying to create a curriculum with this work, I do want to focus on using novel and/or essential lessons for students who might require intervention. Figurative language is one of those essential lessons.

Research Background

Interpretive reading is the ability to detect the mood or purpose in a text, as well as the ability to draw conclusions from the material that may not be explicitly stated. According to Burns, Roe, and Smith (2009), the process of figuring out that ideas are often implied rather than directly stated is crucial for literacy within literature.

With literature and reading at the secondary level, students must be able to draw upon schema (prior knowledge) to read interpretively. Interpreting figurative language is an inferential task of higher-order comprehension and vocabulary analysis. Students who are not part of the mainstream culture may struggle with this task (Burns et al., 2009). Teaching students strategies to build their understanding of vocabulary, in a literal and figurative sense, will help overall comprehension and literacy. In addition, their vocabulary development, reading accuracy, and internalization of text will improve.

As stated in a previous section, Reciprocal Teaching and Think-Alouds help students master and grasp the concept of figurative language. Think-Alouds involve verbalizing the mental processes that readers use to construct meaning from written materials (Burns et al., 2009). Used correctly, Think-Alouds follow a format where teachers tell their students what the strategy is, why it is important and helpful, and when to use it. According to Burns et al., instructors can apply this process either explicitly or implicitly. The use of visual aids and graphic organizers contributes to Think-Aloud strategies. They can help students master figurative language literacy and comprehension.

Learning Objectives

- To identify and infer meanings of figurative language within text
- To use Think-Aloud strategies to build mastery of figurative language
- To provide students with the skills and ability to connect with text beyond basic literal comprehension
- To use graphic organizers to discern meanings of figurative language within reading material
- To expand and increase vocabulary of new words

Addresses These Nonresponder Indicators

- The student has difficulty connecting new information with previous knowledge.
- The student's skills are fragile; that is, the student possesses the necessary skills but is not yet fluent and automatic in those skills.
- The student's verbal acquisition is limited (may result from cultural language differences).
- The student has a performance (motivation) deficit: that is, the student has the necessary skills but lacks the motivation to complete the academic task.
- The student has a skill deficit (lacks the necessary skills to perform the academic task).
- The student has difficulty effectively using words to express organized and complete thoughts in writing.
- The student struggles to distinguish between literal and figurative language.
- The student's word usage skills are below standard.

Materials Needed

- A poem or a book-length work of literature. Specifically, *The House on Mango Street*, by Sandra Cisneros, works well.
- K-W-L (What I Know, What I Want to Know, What I Learned) Chart (see Figure 4.9 on page 79), which draws directly upon a student's schemata
- Figurative Language Handout (see Figure 4.10 on page 80)
- Pen and paper
- *Romeo and Juliet* movie

The movies and books used in this sample lesson plan can be interchanged with materials relevant to your classroom.

Approximate Time Frame for Completion

This lesson plan may take more than one class period, depending on class length.

- Whole group strategy: 10- to 15-minute minilessons
- Small group practice: 10 to 15 minutes
- Partner work: 10 to 15 minutes
- One-on-one interventions: 10 to 15 minutes (variable, depending on student need)

Intervention Procedure and Scripts

Tier One: Whole Group

Activity One: Figurative Language

1. Write the words *What, Why, How,* and *When* on the board. Leave enough space to write next to each word.

2. Next to the word *What* write the phrase *figurative language.* Ask students what they think the phrase means. What do they know about figurative language?

3. Give an overview of what figurative language is, and share some examples that are common to the vernacular to your students' lives, communities, or regional slang.

4. Explain how figurative language functions, and write about it next to *How* on the board. Then write and explain when it is used.

5. Have students complete a figurative language K-W-L Chart (Figure 4.9 on page 79) as a group or individually.

6. Come back together as a group to determine what the group knows and wants to know about figurative language.

7. After completing the discussion, explain to the students that there are many types of figurative language used in literature.

Activity Two: Metaphors, Similes, and Idioms

8. Make three columns on the board. Label them *Metaphors, Similes,* and *Idioms.*

9. Write an example underneath each term.
   a. metaphor: He has the heart of a lion.
   b. simile: She was as pretty as a rose.
   c. idiom: Keep your eyes peeled.

10. Explain to the students each type of figurative language listed.

   a. A metaphor describes something by comparing two different things.

   b. A simile describes something by using the words *like* or *as*.

   c. An idiom is a phrase that has a meaning different from its literal meaning. It is difficult to determine whether something is an idiom because it is very similar to a metaphor. The differentiator is that an idiom adds more color and interest to language.

11. As a class, come up with an example of at least one type of figurative language together.

12. Read an excerpt from *The House on Mango Street* by Sandra Cisneros or a book of your choice.

13. As a class, identify figurative language from the passage you read.

14. Assign students to pairs: Use the High with Middle, Middle with Low method of choosing pairs (see Figure 2.5 on page 18).

15. Pass out the Figurative Language Handout (Figure 4.10 on page 80) to each student in the group.

16. Assign each pair a chapter to read from *The House on Mango Street* or your chosen text. Chapters should be very short and easy to read.

17. Instruct one student to take notes and identify figurative language (metaphors, similes, and idioms) as his or her partner reads.

18. Have students read their chapter and discuss examples of the three types of figurative language they found in their reading. Students will record their findings on the handout.

Tier One: Whole Group

1. Have one person from each pair share at least one example of figurative language from their reading with the class. Ask the students to write the figurative statement on the board and tell the class what type of language they thought it was.

2. After each group has shared, randomly review other findings with the class. For example, select a particular statement and as a class determine what type of figurative language it is and why.

3. Select groups to read their examples of figurative language. Have the rest of the class guess if it is a metaphor, simile, or idiom.

4. Randomly prompt students about figurative language to check for internalization within the discussion.

Tier Two: Small Group (May Also Be Used at Tier One)

1. As a class, watch a portion of a film version of *Romeo and Juliet* or any literature-based movie of your choice. Play using the closed-caption feature so students can more easily identify figurative language in the movie while watching.

2. Have students write down figurative language as it occurs in the movie. You may need to replay scenes for students to write down and internalize the material.

3. Assign students to small groups of four students. Use the High with Middle, Middle with Low grouping strategy (see Figure 2.5 on page 18). Each group will need the Figurative Language Handout (Figure 4.10 on page 80) and paper to take notes.

4. In groups, have students complete the Figurative Language Handout on two pieces of figurative language from the movie.

5. Have the students come up with at least three examples of figurative language for each type learned in the lesson, write them down, and swap papers with another group.

6. Have each group try to guess what type of figurative language each of the other group's examples are. The group should complete a handout for at least two of the types of figurative language that they guessed the implied meaning of.

Tier Three: One on One

1. Students work with a specialist or one on one with the teacher to master the skill.

2. Start by writing out examples of metaphors, similes, or idioms on index cards or a whiteboard. If using a whiteboard, write them on a separate sheet of paper and transfer them to the whiteboard one at a time. Make sure to have a variety of examples available. .

3. Introduce an example.

4. Have the student read it aloud.

5. Student must determine what type of figurative language it is and why.

6. Provide correction and explanation as needed.

7. Increase difficulty as student progresses.

8. Repeat until the student reads at least 10 examples and reaches 80% mastery.

9. End with the student reading a portion of House on Mango Street or other reading and completing a Figurative Language Handout (Figure 4.10 on page 80) on one piece of figurative language from the book.

To Differentiate

- Work at developmental or reading level of students.
- Have students read a simple poem and pull out figurative language.
- Show an excerpt from movies about the same topic to show examples of figurative language. Try Romeo and Juliet, Grapes of Wrath, Gone with the Wind, or Robin Hood.

- Have students write a basic story. Then have them enhance the piece with figurative language. If students are capable of writing the piece with figurative language on the first edit, that is fine. Many students, however, will be stymied if they try to focus on elaboration in the creation phase.
- Have students create riddles. This helps them write about inferences and figurative language.

Assessment

Rubric: Figurative Language Handout

Category	1	2	3	4
Overall Practice	Makes no attempt to complete the handout or participate.	Correctly completes three steps and identifies figurative language.	Correctly completes four steps and identifies figurative language.	Correctly completes five steps and signs all of the words. • Writes the appropriate type of figurative language in the box. • Identifies it correctly. • Writes a statement as to what they thought it meant literally and nonliterally. • Draws a picture representing the word accurately. • Comes up with a new figurative language statement.
Writing	Uses fragmented or incomplete sentences.	Inadequately describes what the meaning is.	Uses an adverb and adjective to describe meaning.	Uses adjectives and adverbs to describe meaning and new figurative language statement.
Picture	Gives no detail or creativity to depict the word.	Uses some detail or creativity to depict the word.	Uses creative imagery and shows thought.	Is very creative and demonstrates meaningful thought.
Vocabulary Assessment	Correctly identifies figurative language less than 70% of the time.	Correctly identifies figurative language at least 70% of the time.	Correctly identifies figurative language at least 80% of the time.	Correctly identifies figurative language at least 90% of the time.

Across the Curriculum

Social studies, science, or math teachers can use this approach to have their students master concept-specific vocabulary.

- Establish a context for figurative language in a social studies lesson by watching a historical movie or by reading books from a specific time period. Note whether the metaphors, similes and idioms used are indicative of the period in history.
- Give examples of figurative language in math word problems. There are many times when instructions call for the nonliteral interpretation of items and solutions.
- Demonstrate figurative language in science. It is used often to describe plants and animals.

Vocabulary Interventions

- Have ELL/ESL students read figurative language in their native language or in a text related to their native culture. Students that are not from the mainstream culture can struggle with metaphors and idioms more than other students. Introduce similes first and then move to more complex types of figurative language.
- Utilize pictures and cartoons to describe figurative language.

Extension Learning

Instead of working generically, focus on one type of figurative language at a time and provide books, texts, or movie clips that push students to take their understanding to a deeper level. The premise is that more intense and focused practice of the skill yields a higher mastery level.

■ HIGHER-ORDER COMPREHENSION

There are so many higher-order thinking skills required of students that one could write an entire book of lesson plans on the topic. For this lesson I've chosen separating fact from opinion.

This skill is particularly important because of the proliferation of altered truths circulating the Internet through e-mail and website propaganda. Too many people take too many of these claims to be factual because they are in written form, when, in reality, they are merely opinion.

Students need to learn to distinguish fact from opinion. They need to learn to question what they read, research the issue, and discover the truth. The skill of identifying fact from opinion is also necessary for higher-order comprehension as well as for increasing students' state test scores. Learning to discern what is true from what is false so that one's decisions are based on correct information is a critical life skill.

Research Background

Comprehension

Comprehension is the literal recall of information from a read text. *Higher-order comprehension* goes beyond the literal understanding of material and connects with students' higher-order thinking skills. Incorporating higher-order comprehension into lesson plans at the secondary level is crucial for proper development of skills at analysis and synthesis. As students advance in their studies, reading progresses from simple recall and recitation of facts to in-depth inferential analysis of material.

Implementing higher-order comprehension skills into instruction helps prepare students to analyze material while they read. Students learn how to read critically, which requires them to evaluate written material and compare the ideas discovered there with known standards to draw conclusions (Burns et al., 2009). This critical reading allows students to use higher-order thinking skills and to apply them to information presented within text.

Fact or Opinion

Looking at material and determining if it is fact or opinion allows students to comprehend material in an objective fashion. Learning to differentiate between fact and opinion statements while reading helps students to develop critical reading strategies that foster higher-order comprehension skills (Burns et al., 2009). When students make this connection, they look beyond the literal meaning of statements and read critically, thus improving comprehension.

Learning Objectives

- To develop higher-order comprehension strategies to understand and interpret text
- To practice the differentiation of fact from opinion statements
- To provide students with the skills and ability to connect with text beyond basic literal comprehension
- To connect Bloom's taxonomy to the evaluation of texts read within the classroom

Nonliteral language includes metaphor, idioms, and other figurative language. For example, a writer might be extremely tired, yet rather than speak literally and say, "I'm extremely tired," the writer states, "I'm dead on my feet." An example of nonliteral interpretation might be: "I breathe fire when I'm angry!" If interpreted literally, a student will think that a person actually breathed fire. If the student understands the nonliteral interpretation, they will understand that rather than actually breathing fire, the person was extremely angry and his angry behavior would appear terrifying to anyone around him.

Addresses These Nonresponder Indicators

- The student has difficulty connecting new information with previously learned knowledge.
- The student has language difficulties; specifically, with differentiating between fact and opinion and with interpreting figurative language.
- The student has difficulty effectively using words to express organized and complete thoughts in writing.

- The student's word usage skills are below standard; specifically, has difficulty recognizing context cues that might distinguish fact from opinion.
- The student's ability to compare and contrast is weak, specifically from web-based sources.
- The student struggles to provide adequate evidence when stating drawing conclusions.

Materials Needed

- Any newspaper with an editorial or opinion section
- At least one news article from the paper
- At least one opinion article from the paper
- Fact Versus Opinion Handout (see Figure 4.11 on page 81)
- News video (any video on news from your local news station; they are easy to find online)
- News blog or entertainment blog (video is preferred; however, anything that illustrates the concept of opinion will work)
- A famous person's official website and a fan-made website: print out information from each site if students cannot access the Internet during group instruction

The choice of reading material and videos to be used is flexible. The idea is to find two types of information from which students can determine and identify fact and opinion.

Approximate Time Frame for Completion

This lesson plan may take more than one class period, depending on class length.

- Whole group minilessons: 30 to 40 minutes
- Tier Two and Tier Three practice: Each 10 minutes or less, depending on available time and reading length and quantity of reading
- Extension learning: Time is variable; analyze more articles for time extension or news on a daily basis for extension learning

Intervention Procedure and Scripts

Tier One: Whole Group

1. Discuss a news item with the class. This can be an article from the newspaper or a news video. Make sure it is a current or recent event. Showing the recast of the prior evening's news from a website is a great way to grab the attention of students. Discussing stories on the front page of the paper will also work.

2. Guide students in a discussion about the newscast or news article chosen. Create two columns on the board titled *What we know* and *What we thought*.

3. Ask students to tell you things they know about the story.

4. Create a bulleted list of approximately five things they learned (*What we know*). These should be facts, but do not explicitly state this. For example, if the story was about a car accident they can state, "There was a car accident on Interstate 10 yesterday."

5. In the *What we thought* column, have students give you five statements about what they thought about the story; for example, "The person in the accident must have been texting" or "They weren't paying attention, because that is an easy highway to drive."

6. After completing the list, point out that the first column lists facts about the story, while the second column is what they thought about the story, or opinions.
   a. Explain that a fact is a true statement about what happened in a story or about a piece of information.
   b. Explain that an opinion is one's own individual thought about something and not a fact.

7. Discuss why it is important when reading to discern fact from opinion.

8. Explain that as they read they need to be able to determine if something is a fact or an opinion instead of looking at the information for what it literally means. For example, point out a fact from the list and tell the students that when you read this fact it tells you exactly what happened. However, when you read an opinion, you see that someone is expressing a personal feeling or perspective about something.

9. Write the following words on the board: *believe*, *may*, *seems*, *think*, *appears*, *probably*, *likely*, and *possibly*. Point out that these are key indicators of opinionated statements.

10. Read an excerpt from a news article in the paper and an excerpt from an editorial to illustrate fact and opinion. Have students verbally identify the opinion from the fact by listening for the key indicators from Step 9.

Note: Some students have trouble developing higher-order comprehension skills or reading critically at their appropriate level because they have trouble differentiating between fact and opinion or lack a clear idea of what a fact is. Developing this skill allows them to understand text better since many authors use these statements intermittently within writing and literature.

Tier One/Tier Two: Small Group

1. Assign students to pairs or small groups of three to four students: Use the High with Middle, Middle with Low grouping strategy (see Figure 2.5 on page 18).

2. Have students work at computers to explore two different celebrity websites. If this is not possible, print out the content of the website ahead of time and give a copy to each group.

3. Explain to students that they need to go through the website (either online or hard copy) and identify facts and opinions.

4. Have them record their findings on the Fact Versus Opinion Handout (Figure 4.11 on page 81).

5. On a separate sheet of paper, have students determine why they came up with their assertions and be prepared to defend them.

6. Have students then determine why a biography or a website about someone can include opinion, exaggeration, and elaboration, as well as facts. Have them discuss this and note their ideas on a piece of paper.

Tier One: Whole Group

1. Have a person from each group share one fact and one opinion from the website.

2. Write their thoughts on the board in the two-column approach used within your initial instruction and analysis of the news video: *What we know* and *What we thought*.

3. After each group has shared their facts and opinions, randomly review some with the class. For example, look at some of the statements identified as facts and determine if they are truly fact, or if they are opinion (or figurative language).

4. Look at some of the information from each website to see if fact and opinion are on both.

5. Demonstrate to students that they are critically reading information on the site and looking into text for nonliteral meanings.

6. Follow up by having students identify facts and opinions from another news article and from another opinion piece to determine whether they have internalized the concepts.

7. Randomly prompt students to identify fact and opinion statements.

Tier Two: Small Group (May Also Be Used at Tier One)

1. Put students in mixed-ability groups of two or three. Use the High with Middle, Middle with Low grouping strategy (see Figure 2.5 on page 18).

2. Each group will need a news or opinion article. Make sure that students cannot determine what type of article they have by simply glancing at it.

3. As students read their articles, instruct them to underline key indicators that indicate an opinion is being expressed. Have them circle statements that they believe are facts.

4. Have students write down at least three statements that help determine if they have a factual or an opinion article.

5. When reading is complete, come together and discuss findings. Help students determine what type of article they had and if it was fact or opinion.

6. Have students write at least two random facts or opinions, and then have them prompt other students within the group. Monitor this activity, listening for mastery. Correct as needed to ensure that students internalize the skill.

Tier Three: One on One

1. Students work with a specialist or one on one with the teacher to master the skill.

2. Start by writing out statements on index cards or a whiteboard. If using a whiteboard, write statements on a separate sheet of paper and transfer them to the whiteboard one at a time. Make sure to have a variety of facts and opinions. Increase difficulty as you progress with instruction. For example:
   - Facts: The sky is blue. February is the second month of the year. Dogs have tails.
   - Opinions: Purple is the best color. Spaghetti is gross. Watching TV at night is not productive.

3. Introduce a statement.

4. Have the student read the statement aloud.

5. The student must determine if the statement is fact or opinion and state why.

6. Provide correction and explanation as needed.

7. Increase in difficulty as the student progresses.

8. Repeat until the student reads at least 10 statements and reaches 80% mastery.

9. End with the student reading a news article and an opinion article. Have them point out facts and opinions in both.

To Differentiate

- Work at developmental and reading level of students.
- Have students read biographies written about someone by two different people.
- Show excerpts from movies about the same topic. For example, *Flags of Our Fathers* and *Letters from Iwo Jima* provide two perspectives of World War II, and each contains both fact and opinion.

- Have students write about a specific sport or animal. Have them write five facts and five things that they either like or do not like about the sport or animal. Then have them switch with a partner and find the facts and opinions.
- Have them read news blogs and news websites for a period of one week and identify fact and opinion from the sites.

Assessment

Rubric: Fact Versus Opinion Handout

Category	1	2	3	4
Overall Practice	Made no attempt to complete the handout or look for opinions and facts in the article.	Attempted to complete the handout and made minimal effort within the group.	Completed the handout and made efforts to help find facts and opinion within the reading and discussion.	Correctly completed the work sheet and 1. wrote topic in center box and what they know about it. 2. identified opinions and facts in the articles and discussions. 3. demonstrated proficiency in the assignment. 4. contributed actively to the discussions and class work as a whole.
Writing	Sentences are fragmented or incomplete.	Provides minimal explanation and use of sentences on assignment.	Clearly explains and identifies what the topic is, opinions, and facts. Writes proficient and complete sentences.	Clearly explains and identifies what the topic is and opinions and facts in a superior fashion. Writes proficient and complete sentences that are free from grammatical and syntax errors.
Critical Reading Applications	Identifies fact and opinion less than 70% of the time when prompted.	Identifies fact and opinion at least 70% of the time when prompted.	Identifies fact and opinion at least 80% the time when prompted.	Identifies fact and opinion at least 90% of the time when prompted.

Across the Curriculum

Social studies, science, or math teachers can use this approach to have their students master concept-specific vocabulary.

1. Have students find facts and opinions in scientific theories and journals while reading.

2. Have students read about personal perspectives within social studies, such as perspectives on laws and bills in government, military involvement, or any other social issue in the current news.

3. Write an opinion piece or news article on a subject or concept you are studying in any subject.

Vocabulary Interventions

Have ELL/ESL students read an article in their native language or from within their culture to discern facts and opinions in a context they already understand. Then have them practice within American culture and English to make the connection.

ADDITIONAL INTERVENTIONS ■
FOR READING COMPREHENSION

Ask Questions

Another effective strategy is to ask questions at the end of a reading. Have a template with questions like

- Has anything like this ever happened to me?
- Did I ever feel this way? (The brain remembers what's emotional.)
- Does this happen in my neighborhood?

At the end of each reading, have students answer a question in their journal or notebook, or tell a partner the answer. Verbally sharing a response is ideal for students for whom writing an answer might be too difficult. Also, use this strategy for homework. Send a list of questions home with a reading assignment and have students answer the questions with a parent or sibling who can scribe their answer.

Storyboards as an Intervention

To make a storyboard, have students fold a piece of paper into squares and draw about what they read. They might do this while they read a story for the first time, as a review with a partner, or for homework after a reading assignment. The process of turning verbal information into a visual format reinforces the learning and keeps the information in working memory longer (Fitzell & Fitzell, 2006).

Intervention for Difficulty Sequencing: Sequencing Strips

To remember information in sequence, such as a timeline in history, a cycle in science, or the chronology of a story, use adding machine tape or strips of paper and have students draw their storyboard in sequence. Now they can see the sequence of the storyline, timeline, or process literally in visual, sequential format (Figure 4.1).

Figure 4.1   Sequencing Strip Example Based on Albert Camus' Book *The Plague*.

Figure 4.2

Summary Graphic Organizer

What happened at the beginning?

_____
_____
_____
_____
_____
_____

↓

What happened in the middle?

_____
_____
_____
_____
_____
_____

↓

What happened at the end?

_____
_____
_____
_____
_____
_____

Figure 4.3 SWBS Table Graphic Organizer

Somebody	
Wanted	
But	
So	

Figure 4.4   Beginning, Middle, and End

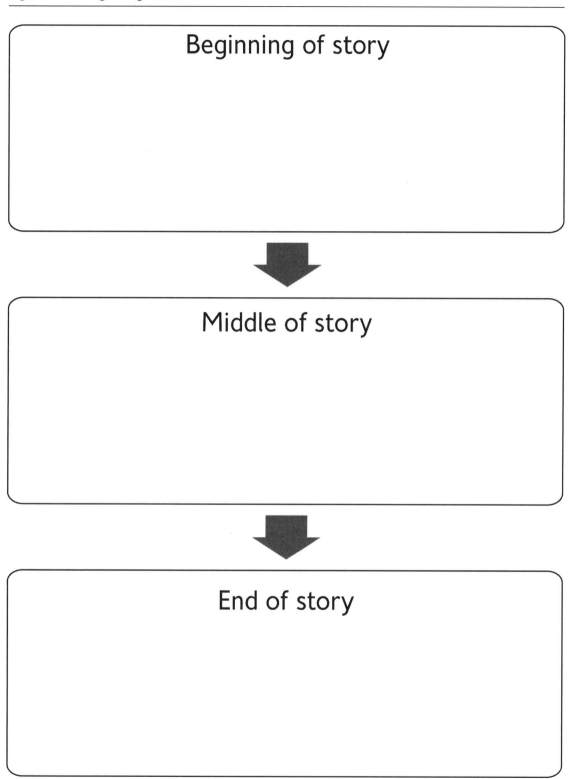

Figure 4.5 Questioning Web

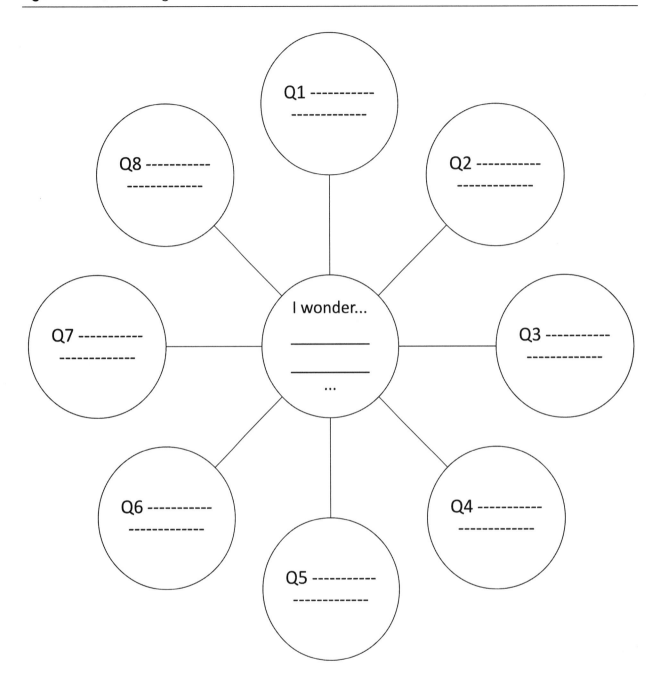

Figure 4.6 QAR Bookmark

 Types of Questions "Hint" Bookmark

 **Right There**
(Find your answer in the text.)

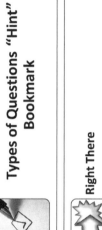 **Think & Search**
(Search for the answer in the text and also synthesize it.)

 On My Own
(Answer based on your own experiences and knowledge.)

 Author and Me
(The answer is inferred within the text. Combine what you read with what you know to answer.)

 **Types of Questions "Hint" Bookmark**

 **Right There**
(Find your answer in the text.)

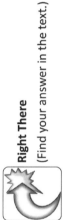 **Think & Search**
(Search for the answer in the text and also synthesize it.)

 **On My Own**
(Answer based on your own experiences and knowledge.)

 **Author and Me**
(The answer is inferred within the text. Combine what you read with what you know to answer.)

 **Types of Questions "Hint" Bookmark**

 **Right There**
(Find your answer in the text.)

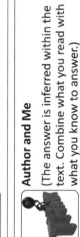 **Think & Search**
(Search for the answer in the text and also synthesize it.)

 **On My Own**
(Answer based on your own experiences and knowledge.)

Author and Me
(The answer is inferred within the text. Combine what you read with what you know to answer.)

Figure 4.7 QAR Graphic Organizer

Types of Questions Graphic Organizer

Right There

(Find your answer in the text.)

Think & Search

(Search for the answer in the text and also synthesize it.)

On My Own

(Answer based on your own experiences and knowledge.)

Author and Me

(The answer is inferred within the text. Combine what you read with what you know to answer.)

Figure 4.8

Name _____

Date _____

CODING PICTURE BOOKS

Title _____

Author _____

Subject _____

Why I chose this book

What I learned

Facts

Interesting Information

Further Questions

(Continued)

(Continued)

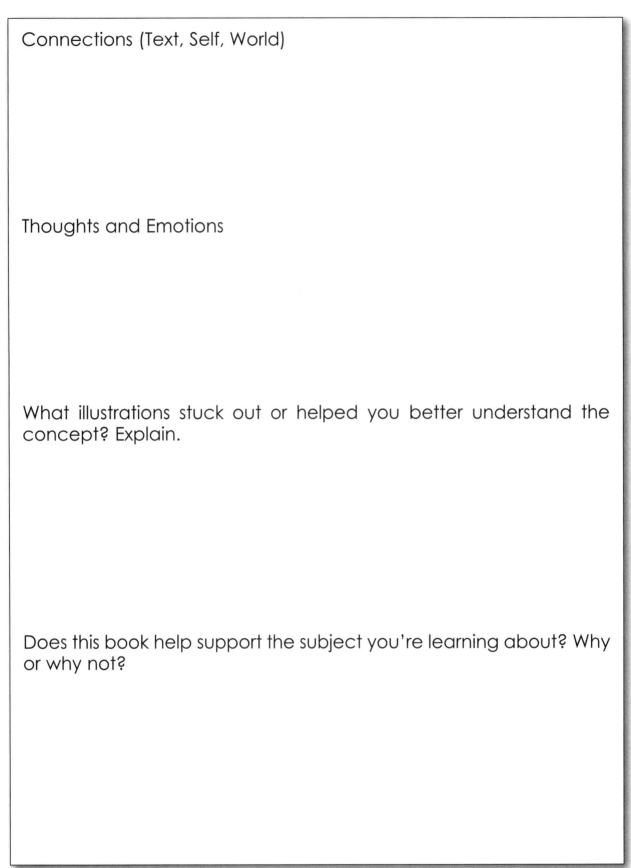

Connections (Text, Self, World)

Thoughts and Emotions

What illustrations stuck out or helped you better understand the concept? Explain.

Does this book help support the subject you're learning about? Why or why not?

Figure 4.9 K-W-L Chart

What I **K**now . . .	What I **W**ant to Know . . .	What I **L**earned About . . .

Figure 4.10 Figurative Language Handout

Type of Figurative Language	Phrase

What I think it means . . . figuratively

What it means . . . literally

My New Phrase

Picture

Figure 4.11   Fact Versus Opinion Handout

Facts

_____

_____

_____

_____

_____

_____

Topic

_____

What we know

_____

_____

_____

_____

Opinions

_____

_____

_____

_____

_____

_____

5

Writing Intervention Strategies

■ WRITING PARAGRAPHS: GROUPING AND ORGANIZING INFORMATION

Using the Friendly Letter as an Approach to Improving Writing Skills

Several years ago, when I was teaching science, I searched for a way to teach students citizenship and environmental awareness, and at the same time to improve their writing skills. I had them research an environmental issue they felt passionate about. After they decided on an issue and did some research on the topic, I instructed them to research whether any bills were in process to address the issue. If not, they were to find out to whom to write to call attention to the issue. If there was a bill in place, they needed to write to their state representative and encourage them to vote on the bill. Then they wrote a letter to that key person and actually mailed it.

I stressed how important it was to write a professional-looking letter. I explained that their letter not only represented them, but it also represented the school. We did not want to embarrass the school. The students took the issue and the project very seriously. One of my students decided to go straight to the top. He wrote to then First Lady Barbara Bush. This student, Charles, also happened to be my most challenging student in the class, behaviorally and academically.

On the last day of school, I was packing up my classroom. Suddenly, I heard my name shouted in the hallway in an excited chant. "Mrs. Fitzell!

Mrs. Fitzell! Mrs. Fitzell." I recognized the voice. It was Charles. Eventually, he burst into the room waving a piece of paper. "Mrs. Fitzell, look, look! I got an answer from Mrs. Bush!" He shoved the paper in front of my face excitedly. "Look!" I oooed and ahhhed and praised him for doing such a great job on that letter. We talked about the assignment and how hard he worked on it. I'll never forget the pride on his face. That is what a teacher lives for.

Research Background

The creation of a graphic organizer in a small group is an active and collaborative learning exercise. Because a graphic organizer captures a specific topic in a nonlinear fashion and incorporates pictures and colors, this exercise also can connect with learners whose style is not well served by traditional linear, text-based materials (Hyerle, 2009; Marzano, Paynter, Kendall, Pickering, & Marzano, 1991; Marzano et al., 2001; O'Donnell & King, 1999; Pehrsson & Denner, 1989).

Learning Objectives

- To organize information according to a theme
- To write a friendly letter in the proper format
- To support the main idea of a paragraph
- To use appropriate questioning to find additional information

Addresses These Nonresponder Indicators

- The student has Attention Deficit Disorder.
- The student's word usage skills are below standard.
- The student has difficulty organizing information.
- There have been gaps in the student's instruction in writing skills.
- The student is unable to set writing goals or has inattention and regulation problems when writing.
- The student has low clerical aptitude or difficulty completing written work.
- The student has notetaking deficiencies.
- The student struggles to use words effectively to express organized and complete thoughts in writing.

Materials Needed

- A selection of books from popular authors
- Rubric
- Friendly letter parts on strips of paper in an envelope
- Appropriate titles for the letters in each envelope
- Friendly Letter Graphic Organizer (see Figure 5.9 on page 97)
- Colored pencils or markers
- Note cards

Approximate Time Frame for Completion

This lesson plan may take more than one class period, depending on class length.

- Whole group strategy (friendly letter kinesthetic activity): 5 minutes
- Main whole group activity: 15 minutes
- Small group practice: 10 to 15 minutes (variable, depending on class dynamics and level of student participation)
- Partner work: 10 to 15 minutes
- Independent practice and peer feedback: 10 to 15 minutes (variable, depending on article length and student understanding)

Intervention Procedure and Scripts

Tier One: Whole Group

Introduction to Friendly Letter

The following kinesthetic memory strategy is perfectly appropriate for sixth and seventh graders. Whether a teacher can pull it off in Grades 8 through 12 depends on the dynamics of the class and the teacher's approach.

Review the parts of a friendly letter with your students using the following movement strategy.

- Stand up and touch their heads for the letter heading.
- Wave for the greeting.
- Do a silly pose with their bodies for the body of a letter.
- Have them pretend to slam a door for the closing.
- Then have students sign their names in the air for the signature of the letter.

Tier One: Small Group

1. Collect samples of friendly letters as a precursor to this activity.

2. Photocopy the letters and cut the copies into strips that represent each part of the letter: heading, greeting, body paragraphs, closing, and signature.

3. Place each group of letter parts in an envelope.

4. Assign students to small groups of four students. Use the High with Middle, Middle with Low grouping strategy (see Figure 2.5 on page 18).

5. Hand out one of the envelopes to each group.

6. Provide each group, or the whole class, with a list of titles to use in their letters.

7. Instruct each group to put their letter together in order and attach the appropriate titles. This can be a timed activity if it will be fun for the students and not cause them undue stress.

8. Walk around and monitor student work.

Time Modification for Tier One/Small Group

Give each group one part of the friendly letter and one title. Have them work with other groups to copy or stick the parts of the letter on the board in proper order.

Tier One: Whole Group

1. Explain to the students that they are going to write a letter to their favorite author using the friendly letter format (see Figure 4.10 on page 98).

2. On the board, brainstorm a list of the students' favorite authors and their books using a web-style graphic organizer. Write the words *Favorite Authors* in the center. Then write the authors' names in one color and the books they have written in another.

3. Explain to the students that they will write a letter to an author of their choice expressing something they enjoyed, learned, or felt while reading the book. They will also ask the author questions to promote continued interaction.

4. Hand out the Friendly Letter Graphic Organizer (Figure 5.9 on page 97) and complete an example letter filling in each part of the graphic organizer on the board using student input. Then walk around and assist the students as they complete their individual organizers.

Tier Two/Partner Work

1. Have students use their Friendly Letter Graphic Organizer (Figure 5.9 on page 97) to write letters to their favorite authors. Remind them that this is the rough draft.

2. Students check their drafts against the rubric and edit as necessary as appropriate. Some students may need support with using the rubric.

3. Students then exchange their self-edited letters and rubrics with their partner and peer edit.

4. After each pair has edited their work, they either schedule conference time with the teacher or make an audio recording for the teacher to review.

5. Students work on final drafts incorporating teacher feedback.

Tier Three

Follow the instructions above for partner work and include the support of a specialist. Allow additional time to practice the skills required to complete the steps. A Tier Three strategy would include graphic organizers, creating drafts, partner or teacher editing, and a final draft for all writing exercises so that the process becomes internalized. Give students adequate time to complete writing activities so that they can move through each step unrushed.

To Differentiate

- Students could work in same ability groups.
- Offer choices: Allow students to choose a different recipient. For example, students might choose a politician, actor, musician, or other renowned individual.

Across the Curriculum

- Social studies teachers can use this approach to have the students write friendly letters to historical characters as if they were a friend who lived in that time.
- Science teachers can use friendly letters to write letters to a favorite scientist or inventor. My personal favorite is to write a letter to a state representative regarding an environmental issue about which the student is passionate.
- Math teachers can use friendly letters as writing prompts on math terminology. Their letters simply take what would normally be a short answer response and personalize it. For example, a line graph writes a letter to the Graph family and explains why "he" is related to the bar graphs and circle graphs in the family.

Extension Activities

Students might choose one of the following:

- Write an alternate ending to their favorite book.
- Write a review of their favorite book.
- Draw an alternate cover for their favorite book.

For Independent Reading

Have students read another book by their favorite author, and compare and contrast the two.

The students may create a minibiography about their favorite author or pretend they are a reporter and write a script depicting an interview with their favorite author.

Assessment

Friendly Letter Rubric

Category	1	2	3	4
Neatness and Presentation	Is illegible in many places, numerous author and book-related words are misspelled.	Is sloppy, with several author or book-related words misspelled.	Is neat and orderly in overall appearance and format.	Margins are present on all four sides and text is visually centered at top
	Has more than one section (heading, greeting, body, closing, and signature) missing or out of order.	Has one or more sections (heading, greeting, body, closing, and signature) missing, out of order, or not in proper format.		and bottom. Spacing follows correct friendly letter format with spaces between paragraphs.
Letter Parts	Has three or fewer letter parts.	Has four of the five letter parts.	Has date, greeting, body, closing, and signature.	Has heading, greeting, body, closing, and signature.
Conventions	Punctuation, spelling, and grammar significantly distract the reader. There are more than ten errors.	Punctuation, spelling, and grammar slightly distract the reader. There are seven errors or fewer.	Very good punctuation, spelling, and grammar with fewer than five errors.	Excellent punctuation, spelling, and grammar with fewer than three errors.
Understanding	An introduction, relevant comments about the author's work, or appropriate questions are missing.	Introduction is weak, comments are irrelevant, or the questions are generic.	Letter includes an introduction, relevant comments about the author's work, and asks good questions.	Letter includes specific comments about the author's work, asks excellent questions, has three or more paragraphs, and encourages a response from the reader.

USE CLUSTERING TO ORGANIZE WRITING ■

I have spent years watching students attempt to start a written assignment with an introductory sentence and observing the frustration they experienced because they could not generate that first important sentence. One day, while working with a student named Jamie, I drew a circle and wrote the topic of the essay in the center of the circle. Then I encouraged Jamie to come up with as many words as possible about the topic. "Just tell me what pops into your head!" I coaxed. After we had a circle full of words, I faced another challenge: turning those words into sentences, then into paragraphs. So I took scrap pieces of lined paper and handed Jamie one piece. "Pick a word." This is how the Clustering Writing activity started. I realized that students would get overwhelmed with the big picture idea of writing a whole essay. The sense of being overwhelmed by the task seemed to stop many students cold. However, if I broke the task into chunks by having them write first one word at a time, then one sentence, then one paragraph, and so on until all the pieces were written, students could successfully put them together. Each step of the way, they experienced success through what they accomplished. Instead of looking at a paragraph as so little done, they would look at a paragraph as one more chunk done!

My daughter was struggling with the effort of writing a scholarship application essay during her junior year in high school. I had been using the clustering strategy with students with special needs for years. I had not tried it with an honors-level student. I showed her the technique and suggested she try it. This strategy worked so well for her she continued to use it for all her writing assignments.

Research Background

Graphic organizers have been applied across a range of curriculum subject areas. Although reading is by far the best-studied application, science, social studies, language arts, and math are additional content areas represented in the research base on graphic organizers. In these subject areas, graphic organizers demonstrate benefits that extend beyond their well-established effects on reading comprehension. Operations such as mapping cause and effect, notetaking, comparing and contrasting concepts, organizing problems and solutions, and relating information to main ideas or themes can be broadly beneficial (Ewy, 2003; Marzano et al., 2001; Moore & Readence, 1984).

Learning Objectives

- To organize an essay
- To use specific topic sentences
- To use appropriate sentences to support the topic sentence in each paragraph
- To determine appropriate transition words and phrases to connect paragraphs together (see Figure 5.11 on page 101)
- To complete a well-organized essay

Addresses These Nonresponder Indicators

- The student has Attention Deficit Disorder (finds it a challenge to focus on a writing task to completion).
- The student has difficulty establishing writing goals, or inattention and regulation problems when writing.

- There have been gaps in the student's instruction in writing skills.
- The student has low clerical aptitude (difficulty completing written work).
- The student is paralyzed by anxiety when assigned an essay, paper, or short story.
- The student has problems using a linear outline to complete written assignments.
- The student struggles to use words effectively to express organized and complete thoughts in writing.
- The student is stumped when asked to start a paper by writing the introductory paragraph.
- The student's word usage skills are below standard.

Materials Needed

- One unlined 8.5-by-11-inch sheet of paper per student
- Lined paper strips or lined sticky notes
- Scissors
- Cellophane tape

Approximate Time Frame for Completion

This lesson plan may take more than one class period, depending on class length.

- Whole group strategy (clustering): 30 to 40 minutes
- Tier Two and Tier Three practice: Each 10 minutes or less, depending on available time
- Extension learning: variable

Intervention Procedure and Scripts

Strategy for Getting "Un-Stuck" While Writing: Clustering

The clustering activity detailed on the following pages helps students who are struggling to write an essay, as well as young adults filling out college applications.

Tier One/Whole Group (Introduction)

1. Have your students draw a big circle on a piece of paper, and put the topic of the paper in the center of the circle.

    a. Instruct your students to write any thoughts, ideas, or feelings about the topic in the circle. Students can also ask questions about the topic or draw pictures of ideas.

    b. Do not worry about spelling, grammar, or other conventions at this point. The purpose is to get the ideas out. Worry about writing rules later.

> *Note:* If there is more than one topic, you might have more than one circle. For example, writing about three wishes will require three circles, one for each wish.

Figure 5.1

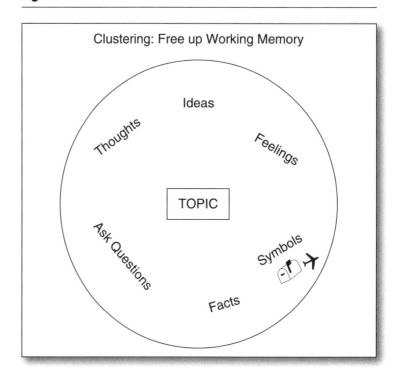

Make this circle *big*—at least the size of an 8" × 8" piece of paper.

2. After students "create" in the circle, allow them to share what they have written with a partner.

Figure 5.2

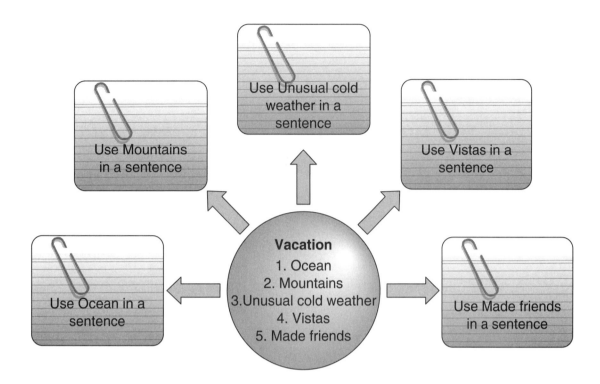

3. Instruct students to take the best words and ideas from inside their circle and use each word in a sentence. These are the topic sentences for the paragraphs they will write.

    a. Write the sentences on strips of lined notepaper or lined sticky notes.

Figure 5.3

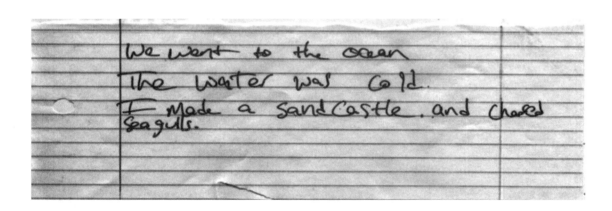

b. Now take each sentence and add some more sentences about the topic sentence on that strip of paper. Try to write two or three more sentences for each topic sentence.

Figure 5.4

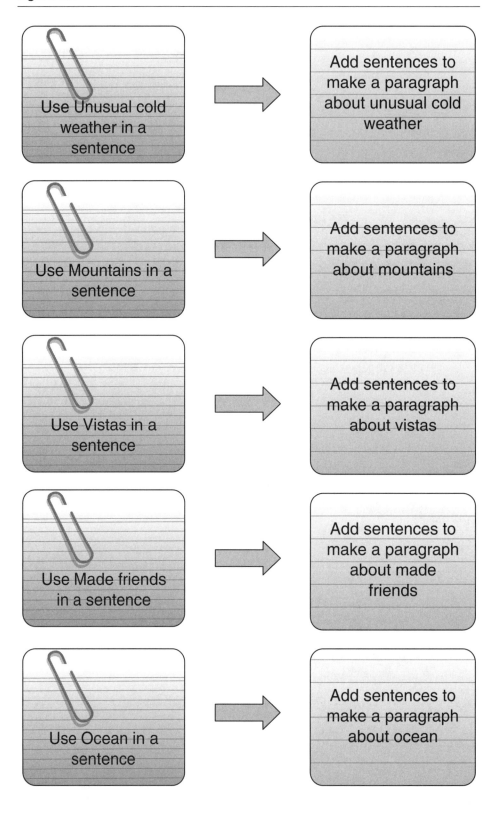

4. Add an introduction and conclusion on separate strips of lined paper.

Figure 5.5

Add sentences to make a paragraph about unusual cold weather

 Add

Add an Introduction

Add sentences to make a paragraph about mountains

Add sentences to make a paragraph about vistas

Add sentences to make a paragraph about made friends

Add sentences to make a paragraph about ocean

 Add

Add a conclusion

Figure 5.6

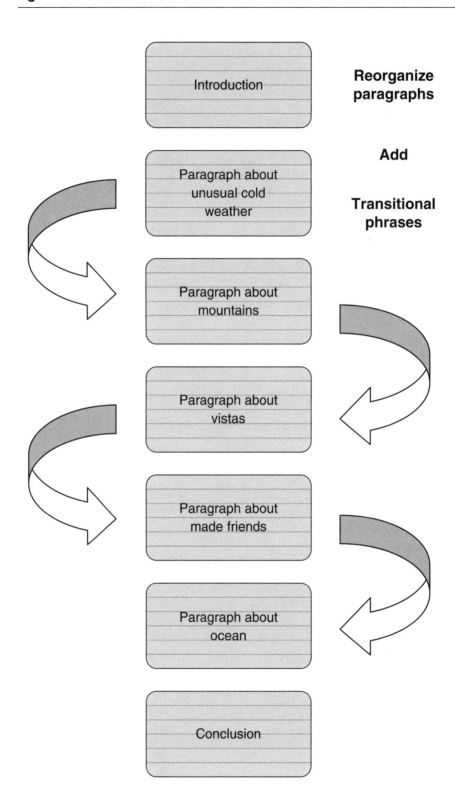

5. Move the strips of paper around so that they are in the best order and make the most sense. This process allows the writer to start anywhere in the paper. It frees up creative thought and encourages the process to start. Organizing the paper after writing paragraphs is easy.

6. Tape all the strips on one or two big pieces of paper.

7. Add transition words to make the paragraphs flow together.

ure 5.7

Introduction

Rewrite or type into one continuous draft on full sheets of paper.

Paragraph about made friends

Hand in draft for the teacher to correct.

If the teacher is not correcting a draft, parents may be able to help with this step.

Paragraph about mountains

Figure 5.8

Paragraph about vistas

Student writes final draft incorporating teacher corrections, feedback, and edits

My Vacation
By Successful Student

Interesting new friends became the focal point of...

The mountains were...

The vistas were inspiring as mountains met the ocean in a clash of green and aquamarine...

Unfortunately, there was an unusual cold weather front...

Overall, the vacation was...

Paragraph about ocean

Paragraph about unusual cold weather

This is when the student uses the rules and makes sure that spelling, grammar, and punctuation are correct.

Conclusion

Tier Two/Tier Three Practice and Interventions

This is an excellent Tier Two and Tier Three practice activity.

1. Take all of the students' strips when they are complete.

2. Put each student's cluster strips in a separate baggie.

3. Have other students place them in order. This can be done as a pair-share, a flexible group activity, or possibly an individual activity with an intervention specialist.

4. Have a copy of the finished essays so they can read them and see if they put them in the same order as the student who wrote the paper.

Across the Curriculum

- Social studies and science teachers can use this strategy to help students write effective essays in their subject areas.
- Math teachers can use it to help students break down and explain multistep problems.

Assessment

Clustering Rubric

Category	1	2	3	4
Neatness and Presentation	Is illegible in many places, with many misspelled words, capitalization errors, and inappropriate spacing.	Is messy in a few spots, with several words misspelled or not capitalized.	Is neat and orderly in overall appearance, with few spelling and capitalization errors.	Is exceptionally neat, orderly, and accurate.
Use of Descriptive Words	Lacks adjectives necessary for visualizing what is happening in the essay.	Shows good choices, but insufficient quantity of adjectives.	Uses descriptive adjectives, helping the reader to visualize what was happening in the essay.	Uses very descriptive adjectives, helping the reader to visualize what was happening in the essay.
Understanding	Is unclear with lots of extraneous information.	Is fairly clear, but supporting sentences do not support the topic sentence and disrupt the flow of the piece.	Is clear with most supporting sentences relevant to the topic sentence.	Is clear with each paragraph containing a topic sentence supported by relevant sentences.

Figure 5.9 Friendly Letter Graphic Organizer

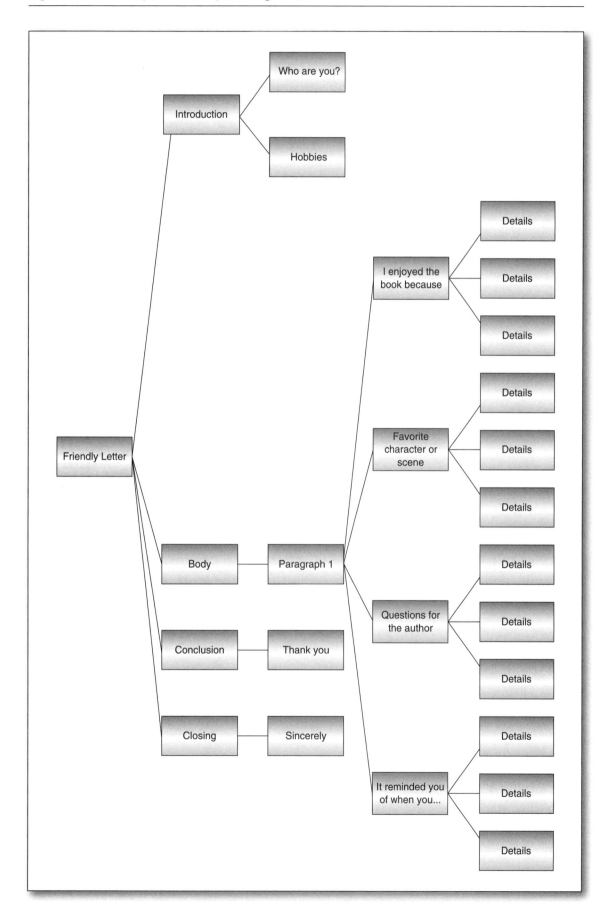

Figure 5.10

FRIENDLY LETTER TEMPLATE

Heading: Make sure you have the correct information on the correct line. It should be on the right side of the paper (see below). You will use the school address.

First line: street number and street name

Second line: town or city, state and ZIP code

Third line: today's date

Let's Get Started

Street Number and Street Name
City or Town, State and Zip Code
Today's Date

Remember your comma!

Greeting or Salutation: Dear (author's first and last name),

_____

_____

Introduction: This part should get the author to want to continue reading and give the author an idea about why you are writing. Tell the author who you are and a little about yourself.

Who are you?

_____

_____

What are your hobbies or interests?

_____

_____

Body: This is the main part of the letter. Ask the author some questions about the book. Ideas: How did you get the idea for this book? Did you base the main character on someone you know? How long did it take you to write this book? Where do you write?

Paragraph 1: Why I liked this book overall.

Write down a strong lead sentence; for example, "I really enjoyed your book *My Sister's Keeper*."

_____

_____

Write down two more things you enjoyed about the book.

_____

_____

_____

_____

Paragraph 2: The character and scenes or events you liked the most.

Write down a strong lead sentence about your favorite character or scene in the book. For example, "Oliver was my favorite because . . . "

_____

_____

Write two more sentences about your favorite character or scene.

_____

_____

_____

_____

_____

_____

_____

(Continued)

(Continued)

Paragraph 3: Questions for the Author

Write down a strong lead sentence. For example, "I would like to know some more about how you write your books."

_____

_____

_____

_____

Write down one or two more questions you have for the author. For example, "Where do you do most of your writing?"

_____

_____

_____

_____

Explain how you connected with the text or the characters.

_____

_____

_____

_____

Conclusion: Wrap it all up and thank the author for his or her time.

_____

_____

_____

_____

Closing: Choose an appropriate closing (*Sincerely, Your fan, Best regards*) and sign your name. Make sure your closing agrees with the heading. Only capitalize the first word.

Signature: Usually in cursive.

Figure 5.11

TRANSITION WORDS

To Add:

and, again, and then, besides, equally important, finally, further, furthermore, nor, too, next, lastly, what's more, moreover, in addition, first (second, etc.)

To Compare:

whereas, but, yet, on the other hand, however, nevertheless, on the other hand, on the contrary, by comparison, where, compared to, up against, balanced against, but, although, conversely, meanwhile, after all, in contrast, although this may be true

To Prove:

because, for, since, for the same reason, obviously, evidently, furthermore, moreover, besides, indeed, in fact, in addition, in any case, that is

To Show Exception:

yet, still, however, nevertheless, in spite of, despite, of course, once in a while, sometimes

To Show Time:

immediately, thereafter, soon, after a few hours, finally, then, later, previously, formerly, first (second, etc.), next, and then

To Repeat:

in brief, as I have said, as I have noted, as has been noted

To Emphasize:

definitely, extremely, obviously, in fact, indeed, in any case, absolutely, positively, naturally, surprisingly, always, forever, perennially, eternally, never, emphatically, unquestionably, without a doubt, certainly, undeniably, without reservation

To Show Sequence:

first, second, third, and so forth. A, B, C, and so forth. Next, then, following this, at this time, now, at this point, after, afterward, subsequently, finally, consequently, previously, before this, simultaneously, concurrently, thus, therefore, hence, next, and then, soon

To Give an Example:

for example, for instance, in this case, in another case, on this occasion, in this situation, take the case of, to demonstrate, to illustrate, as an illustration

To Summarize or Conclude:

in brief, on the whole, summing up, to conclude, in conclusion, as I have shown, as I have said, hence, therefore, accordingly, thus, as a result, consequently, on the whole

6

Math Intervention Strategies

■ **MODEL AND SOLVE EQUATIONS USING MANIPULATIVES**

Using manipulatives is the only way some students can truly understand the concepts being taught in math. Unfortunately, a prevailing myth in secondary education, especially high schools, is that manipulatives are for elementary children only. I am a strong advocate of using manipulatives and concrete representation for teaching math to students at the secondary level, including high school students.

I was always saddened when a new math teacher attempted to use algebra tiles to teach algebraic concepts and then gave up the effort because of negative feedback from either the students or math colleagues. New research in the field promoting a three-pronged approach to teaching math at the secondary level is encouraging. The Concrete Representation Abstract (CRA) approach is a breakthrough in thinking about secondary education.

Again, my goal in this chapter is twofold: First, to provide a sample lesson that teachers will be familiar with, such as the traditional scale activity and to demonstrate how to adapt that lesson to Response to Intervention philosophy; and second, to provide novel, new ideas through a sample lesson using a lesser-known device (geoboards). I also used very simple materials, such as strips of paper, out of consideration for teachers without a huge budget for purchasing manipulatives.

Research Background

Using manipulatives provides students a meaningful context for mathematical knowledge and helps them understand fundamental relationships associated with that knowledge (Witzel & Riccomini, 2010). Multiple embodiments (the use of many different models) allow students to focus on common characteristics and generalize to the abstract. "Helping students make connections between the concrete (e.g., models and manipulatives) and the abstract (e.g., generalizations and symbolic representations) facilitates understanding, promotes success at learning, and helps relieve mathematics anxiety" (Reys, Lindquist, Lambdin, Suydam, & Smith, 2009, p. 17).

In regards to secondary math such as algebra, Henri Picciotto (Picciotto, 2010) writes:

> Even though they cannot make algebra easy, manipulatives can play an important role in the transition to a new algebra course:
>
> - They provide access to symbol manipulation for students who had previously been frozen out of the course because of their weak number sense.
> - They provide a geometric interpretation of symbol manipulation, thereby enriching all students' understanding, and making a powerful connection to another part of mathematics.
> - They support cooperative learning and help improve discourse in the algebra class by giving students objects to think with and talk about. It is in the context of such reflection and conversation that learning happens.

There are four main commercial versions of algebra manipulatives (Picciotto, n.d.). In order of their appearance on the market, they are Algebra Tiles (Cuisenaire), the Lab Gear (Creative Publications), Algeblocks (Southwestern Publishing), and Algebra Models (Classroom Products). All four provide a worthwhile model of the distributive law. However, note that only the Lab Gear and Algeblocks allow work in three dimensions.

Bradley S. Witzel is also an advocate of using manipulatives to teach math through algebra. He describes the Concrete Representation Abstract method (Witzel, 2007). The CRA sequence of instruction consists of teaching students to solve mathematics problems through three levels of instruction, from the manipulation of concrete objects to learning through pictorial representations to finally solving equations through abstract notation (Witzel, 2007).

The CRA approach to teaching mathematics has proven to be beneficial to secondary students with math difficulties in instructional settings ranging from small groups to whole class instruction (Witzel, 2005). In fact, after receiving CRA instruction, students with learning disabilities had a success rate two to three times higher than their traditionally taught peers. According to Witzel, the coauthor of the book *Solving Equations: An Algebra Intervention* (Witzel & Riccomini, 2010), CRA benefits students with math difficulties because it presents information in a multisensory way: visually, auditorily, tactilely, and kinesthetically. This multisensory approach causes the brain to process the information several times in various formats, making it easier for students to memorize, encode, and retrieve the information later. In addition, CRA helps students solve abstract problems even if they cannot think fluently at the abstract level by giving them other levels of learning, both pictorial and concrete, to aid them in solving the problem (Witzel & Riccomini, 2010).

Learning Objectives

- To use manipulatives and symbols to represent situations and solve problems
- To solve linear equations

Addresses These Nonresponder Indicators

- The student has Attention Deficit Disorder.
- The student has difficulty following sequential procedures.
- The student has difficulty with abstract concepts.
- The student is unable to visualize math problems and concepts.
- The student lacks the foundational math skills required for advanced mathematics.
- The student's strategic planning ability is limited.

Materials Needed

- Balance scales
- Pennies or other tokens
- Rubber washers, toothpicks

Approximate Time Frame for Completion

This lesson plan may take more than one class period, depending on class length.

- Whole group strategy: 15 minutes
- Centers and small groups: 10 to 12 minutes each

Intervention Procedure and Scripts

Tier One/Whole group

Model on Balance Scale

1. Put the same number of pennies or tokens on each side of the scale.
   a. Ask students what equation this represents ($n = n$).
   b. In actuality, students may respond, "2 = 2" as opposed to "$n = n$."
   c. If students respond with "2 = 2," then seize the teachable moment to demonstrate how to substitute n as a variable.
   d. Demonstrate that if you subtract the same amount from each side, the scale remains balanced. For example, removing three pennies ($n - 3 = n - 3$) leaves the scale balanced.

2. Place ten pennies or tokens on each side of the scale.

   a. Demonstrate that removing a number of pennies from one side results in an imbalance on the scale. (Removing five from one side results in the equation $n - 5 < n$.)

   b. Remove five tokens from the other side of the scale to achieve a balance again. Then add twelve tokens to one side.

3. In order to make both sides balance again ($17 = 5 + x$), add one penny at a time until the scale balances ($17 = 5 + 12$). Therefore $x = 12$.

4. Demonstrate how to find the value of x by subtracting twelve from both sides of the equation.

5. Model several problems like this. Illustrate the step-by-step solution on the board as you demonstrate the solution process using the scale as a visual example.

Tier One/Tier Two: Partner Activity

1. After modeling to the whole group, assign students to a strategic partnership.

   a. For Tier One: Pair students in a mixed-ability group. Use the High with Middle, Middle with Low grouping strategy (see Figure 2.5 on page 18).

   b. For Tier Two: Pair students in same ability groups and provide 10 minutes of intense coaching while other students are working on their own.

2. Use balance scales with pennies or tokens to practice solving simple linear equations ($x + 3 = 5$; $y + 7 = 9$; $n - 3 = 4$).

3. After students have the opportunity to solve a selection of problems, bring them back together as a group and ask probing questions to ensure understanding and promote critical thinking.

   a. Ask: What did you have to do when you had a subtraction problem rather than an addition problem?

   b. Discuss and reinforce the concept of adding or subtracting the same number from each side.

Centers Application for All Three Tiers

Tier One: Mixed-ability groups

Tier Two: Same ability groups or peer tutoring

Tier Three: Same ability groups with direct, intense coaching by the teacher or math specialist

Investigation Center

In this center, the students will begin to explore dividing both sides of an equation by the same number.

1. Give students a bag with a variety of different kinds of tokens. A sample bag would include five of one item and ten of another (for example, five toothpicks and ten rubber washers).

2. Tell students that the toothpicks and rubber washers are an equation and they need to find out how many rubber washers each toothpick is worth.

3. First, they are to write the equation ($5t = 10w$), then solve it.

4. Have students model the solution of the equation by putting each toothpick on the table, then distributing the rubber washers. In this case, they would put out the five toothpicks. Then, after distributing the rubber washers, they would find that there are two rubber washers for each toothpick.

5. Model how to solve the equation by dividing both sides by five.

Manipulative Center

1. Have students use a scale and tokens in the class to solve linear equations provided by the teacher.

2. Use a virtual scale from a source like The National Library of Virtual Manipulatives (http://nlvm.usu.edu/en/nav/grade_g_4.html). Scroll down to "Algebra Balance Scales" to model and solve linear equations.

Tier Three

Provide intense instruction one on one with a math intervention specialist using activities from the manipulative center. Manipulatives, whether hands-on or virtual, are critical to helping students who struggle with math concepts to gain an understanding. It is also important to allow adequate frequency and time for skill building. Some students simply need more processing time.

Assessment Center

Students show their understanding of linear equations by completing the attached problems. Differentiate these problems by complexity (one-step problems, two-step problems, and challenge problems).

Application Examples

One-Step Problems

$$4 + x = 17$$
$$n - 9 = 13$$
$$3b = 21$$
$$12 + j = 19$$
$$7 - m = 2$$

Two-Step Problems

$$6n + 3 = 21$$
$$2p + 1 = -7$$

$5m - 2 = 18$

$-4y + 3 = -13$

$-2z - 5 = -4$

Challenge Problems

$4x - 5 = 7x + 3$

$2(3n + 4) - (x - 3) = 36$

$3x - 1 = 2x + 7$

Rubric: Using Math Manipulatives and Symbols with Efficacy

Category	1	2	3	4
Student uses manipulatives and symbols to represent situations and solve problems.	At the Teacher Center, student needs consistent support from teacher or peer to translate the items in the manipulative bags into linear equations, write the equations, and solve them.	At the Teacher Center, student translates the items in the manipulative bags into linear equations, writes the equations, and solves them, with teacher support.	At the Teacher Center, student translates the items in the manipulative bags into linear equations and writes the equations with minimal teacher direction. Student solves the equations independently and accurately.	At the Teacher Center, student independently translates the items in the manipulative bags into linear equations, writes the equations, and solves them accurately.
Student solves linear equations.	Student needs support to solve the one-step problems on the practice sheet accurately.	Student solves through the one-step problems on the practice sheet independently and accurately; needs support for two-step problems and longer.	Student solves through the two-step problems on the practice sheet independently and accurately.	Student solves through the "challenge" level problems on the practice sheet independently and accurately.

MULTIPLICATION OF FRACTIONS USING MANIPULATIVES ■

Geoboards are manipulative devices used to illustrate math operations such as fractions and geometry. Originally, they were made of wood with nails driven halfway in, and elastic bands were used to form shapes by wrapping them around the nails. Today, they are available in a variety of designs and materials, including online virtual geoboards, but the basic design of pegs on a board remains. In this lesson we will use a geoboard to provide hands-on, visual representations of fractions.

Engineering professors at Rochester Institute of Technology, Worcester Polytechnic Institute, and Clarkson University have expressed to me their concern over the fact that many of the students in their engineering programs can plug in formulas to solve a math problem on paper, yet these same students cannot apply that math knowledge to building a physical product. Additionally, college-level technical programs all over the country understand and embrace the importance of hands-on practice and the use of manipulatives in their courses. Students at all ability levels need to not only understand abstract mathematical concepts but also the concrete application of those concepts.

Research Background

Several studies show that the long-term use of manipulatives in math produces greater achievement and improves student attitudes (Cebulla, 2000; Grouws & Cebulla, 2000, p. 15) Manipulatives give students objects to think with and talk about, and thus support cooperative learning (Picciotto, n.d.). When students use manipulatives, the teacher can see what mistakes they are making. Furthermore, it gives students the opportunity for multisensory learning, which helps students with high-incidence disabilities (Witzel, 2007).

Learning Objectives

- To use a geoboard as an area model for multiplying fractions, decimals, or percentages
- To teach students how to find the product of two fractions
- To provide students with a visual representation of a mathematical concept
- To teach students how to solve an abstract equation

Addresses These Nonresponder Indicators

- The student has Attention Deficit Disorder.
- The student lacks computational fluency.
- The student has difficulty linking prior knowledge with new information.
- The student has a weak foundation in fractions that impacts higher-level math acquisition.
- The student's skills are fragile; that is, the student possesses the necessary skills but is not yet fluent and automatic in those skills.
- The student has a performance (motivation) deficit: that is, the student has the necessary skills but lacks the motivation to complete the academic task.
- The student has spatial integration-processing difficulties that negatively impact math achievement.

- The student has a skill deficit (lacks the necessary skills to perform the academic task).
- The student struggles to effectively draw an array.
- The student struggles to find the abstract representation of a multiplication problem with fractions.

Materials Needed

- Geoboard
- Rubber bands in three different colors; for example, blue, yellow, red
- Paper and grid paper
- Toothpicks
- Colored pencils or markers

> *Note:* There are a variety of other materials that may be used for these activities, including grid paper, whiteboards, popsicle sticks, etc. We use paper strips and toothpicks in our example simply because these materials are inexpensive as well as easy to obtain and work with.

Approximate Time Frame for Completion

This lesson plan may take more than one class period depending on class length.

- Whole group strategy: 20 minutes
- Tier Two and Tier Three practice:15 minutes
- Tier One interventions: 15 to 20 minutes
- Extension learning: variable

Intervention Procedure and Scripts

Tier One: Whole Group

1. Access prior knowledge through demonstration.
   a. On a virtual geoboard, outline four rows by four rows with a yellow rubber band (Figure 6.1, page 110, Step 1).
   b. Using a red rubber band, show three rows by four rows (horizontally) on the left of the square (Figure 6.1, Step 2).
   c. Connect to new material: Write down the multiplication $\frac{3}{4} \times \frac{3}{4}$ and explain that this question can be read as: What is three quarters $\frac{3}{4}$ of ? Using a blue rubber band on the geoboard, outline another three rows by four rows (vertically) on the bottom of the square (Figure 6.1, Step 3).
   d. The part where the two areas overlap is nine out of sixteen squares. Go on to explain to the students how $\frac{3}{4} \times \frac{3}{4} = \frac{3 \times 3}{4 \times 4} = \frac{9}{16}$, nine units out of the sixteen of the four-by-four square.

Figure 6.1   Geoboard

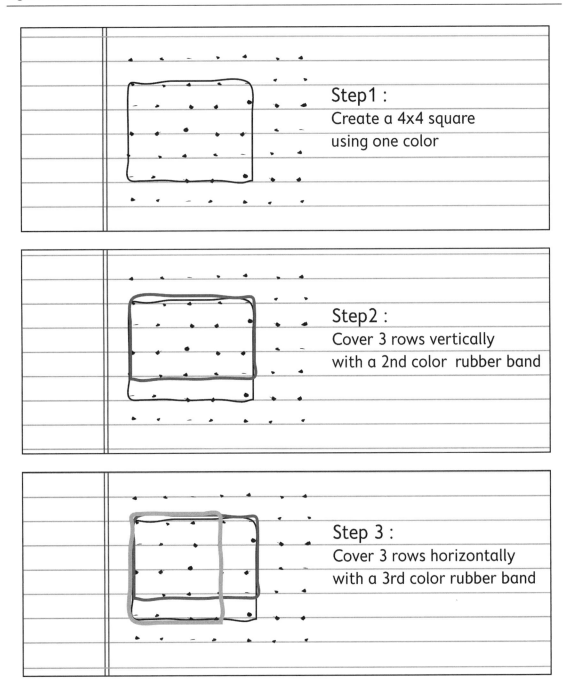

2. Assign students to pairs: Use the High with Middle, Middle with Low grouping strategy (see Figure 2.5 on page 18). Explain to the students that they are going to work with a partner to practice multiplying fractions.

3. Give each pair a geoboard and assign a multiplication problem to them (for example, $\frac{4}{5} \times \frac{1}{2}$ or $\frac{6}{9} \times \frac{1}{3}$). You should assign according to level.

4. Have students use the geoboard to visualize their problem as demonstrated.

5. When all pairs have finished, ask one person from each pair to share their solution with the class.

6. After each presentation also explain to the students how you can calculate each multiplication:

$$\frac{3}{4} \times \frac{3}{4} = \frac{3 \times 3}{4 \times 4} = \frac{9}{16}$$

Tier Two: Small Group (May Also Be Used at Tier One)

1. Put students in mixed-ability groups of two or three. Use the High with Middle, Middle with Low grouping strategy (see Figure 2.5 on page 18). Each group will need paper strips, grid paper, toothpicks, and colored pencils or markers.

2. Use paper strips to make your own mock geoboard out of paper strips and colored toothpicks (Figure 6.2, below).

Figure 6.2 Paper Strip Area Model

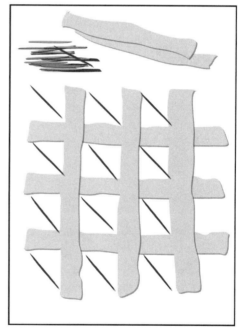

3. Explain that the denominator of each fraction in the multiplication problem determines the horizontal and vertical area of the model. For instance, in Figure 6.2, the denominator would be sixteen because there are four rows and four columns, or sixteen squares.

4. Then use toothpicks to mark parts of the area identified by the numerator of each fraction.

   a. In Figure 6.2, nine of the squares are marked vertically, which would represent $\frac{12}{16}$ or $\frac{3}{4}$.

   b. Just as with the geoboard, students block off the multiplier horizontally using a different color toothpick (Figure 6.2, right).

5. To find the answer, students look at the units that have two toothpicks in them (numerator product) and the total area of the model (denominator product). Assign each group two or three multiplication problems appropriate to their ability.

6. Next, have students draw on grid paper what they did with the paper strips and toothpicks (Figure 6.3). Students will work together to complete the multiplication problems. Each person in the group will complete one problem, draw a visual representation of the problem, and write the abstract equation.

Figure 6.3 Paper Strip Area Model, Multiplying Fraction

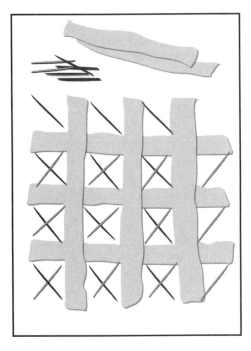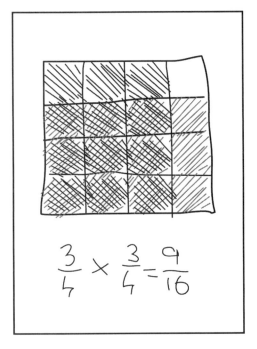

$$\frac{3}{4} \times \frac{3}{4} = \frac{9}{16}$$

Tier Three: One on One

1. Students work with a specialist or one on one with the teacher to master the skill. Instead of a geoboard, try using other manipulatives like cards to represent the units.

2. Provide intense instruction one on one with a math intervention specialist using activities from the manipulative center. Manipulatives, whether hands-on or virtual, are critical to helping students who struggle with math concepts to gain an understanding.

3. It is also important to allow adequate frequency and time for skill building. Some students simply need more processing time.

To Differentiate

• Differentiate by readiness and interest.

You may point out the similarities with multiplication of a fraction with a whole number: $3 \times \frac{6}{8} = \frac{3}{1} \times \frac{6}{8} = \frac{3 \times 6}{1 \times 8} = \frac{18}{8}$.

Make the connection with percentages or decimals.

- Use technology:

National Library of Virtual Manipulatives (http://nlvm.usu.edu). Here you can find a virtual geoboard and a tool to show the multiplication of fractions. Another helpful website is http://www.MathEducationPage.org.

Assessment

Rubric: Multiplication of Fractions Using a Geoboard

Category	1	2	3	4
Uses Geoboard to Solve Equation	Makes no attempt to find either one of the fractions in the multiplication.	Finds both fractions on the geoboard, but does not place them correctly.	Correctly finds both fractions and identifies the area both cover, thus solving the problem. Does not write the abstract equation.	Correctly completes all steps: 1. Finds both fractions. 2. Places correctly on the board (left side and bottom). 3. Finds the correct answer. 4. Draws a representation. 5. Writes the correct equation.

Across the Curriculum

Whether in social studies, science, or math, teachers can use this approach to have their students find part of a part (for example, in recipes and discounts).

GRAPHING LESSON PLAN ■

Not only is the skill of understanding graphs, including reading them, creating them, or critically analyzing them, essential for the secondary math student, it's indispensable to students in English, social studies, science, and most other subjects. As I travel the country and speak to audiences of teachers at the secondary level, one area in math that is universally challenging is the skill of graphing.

Teachers tell me repeatedly that they have to stop their lessons and re-teach how to read graphs every time they encounter one in a lesson, text, handout, or news article. When I ask how long it takes to reteach the process, responses vary from 15 minutes to a full class period.

I not only included this sample lesson plan because of its necessity and familiarity, I would advocate that graphing be a skill that is practiced frequently even as a five-minute minilesson or part of an acceleration center activity.

Research Background

Graphing predictions prior to collecting data helps students evaluate relationships and establishes a foundation for the application of scientific and mathematical principles at their level of achievement. After data collection, students are able to see how their predictions correspond to actual data.

This process leads students to a better understanding of the nature of both science and mathematics. Science and math play a central role in modern culture. This process allows students to see how the two are linked and how these subjects are linked to actual data in everyday applications (Connery, 2007).

Learning Objectives

- To record daily temperature and student absences using a three-column table
- To use a variety of tools to create a scatter plot graph to display data collected
- To determine the type of correlation a scatter plot displays

Addresses These Nonresponder Indicators

- The student has difficulty making connections between data (concrete) and graphs (abstract).
- The student has difficulty visualizing abstract concepts.
- The student's skills are fragile; that is, the student possesses the necessary skills but is not yet fluent and automatic in those skills.
- The student is unable to apply math to real-life situations.
- The student's knowledge and understanding of multistep problems is limited.
- The student has math vocabulary difficulties.
- The student has a performance or motivation deficit (has the necessary skills but lacks the motivation to complete the academic task).
- The student has a skill deficit (lacks the necessary skills to perform the academic task).

Materials Needed

- Ample space to display data charts and scatter plot graphs; a classroom wall would be ideal
- For each student, a manila folder with graph paper (1 cm^2) stapled into the folder for individual data collection and graphing
- Ruler for each student
- Markers, dry-erase markers (if applicable), or colored pencils
- Magnets, Velcro, felt
- Card stock (for the graphs)
- Dry erase boards
- Construction paper
- Cellophane (to make overlays for the graphs)
- Ready-made examples of scatter plot graphs
- Sticky notes
- Round counters (beans, buttons, disks, or similar objects)
- Pegboard, pegs, and overhead transparencies (optional)

Approximate Time Frame for Completion

This lesson can take place in one 60-minute period or two 30-minute segments. The data collection section must be completed during the two weeks prior to the start of the graphing and analysis lesson.

1. Data Collection. Allow 5 to 10 minutes each day for students to record the daily temperature and the number of absences in class. Students should record this information in a chart.

2. Scatter plot creation. This part of the lesson is broken up into two sections:
   a. Whole group instruction: 15 minutes
   b. Small group instruction: 10 minutes per group

3. Data analysis. This part of the lesson is broken up into two sections:
   a. Whole group instruction: 15 minutes
   b. Small group instruction: 10 to 15 minutes per group

Intervention Procedure and Scripts

Tier One: Whole Group (Data Collection)

This lesson should be taught and data collected beginning approximately two weeks prior to the start of the lesson on making graphs.

Note: Students will likely not need intervention at this level, but it is provided below.

1. Find ample resources (newspapers, Internet, and television news) that contain the daily temperature.

2. Create a three-column table model on chart paper that shows the date, the daily temperature, and number of students absent.

3. Model data entry procedures for one day.

Note: Whole group modeling will only be necessary for one day. Students may work in partnerships for the duration of the data collection (see below).

Tier Two: Partner Activity (May Also Be Used at Tier One)

Put students into pairs and record daily data together.

- For Tier One students, these partnerships can be mixed ability.
- For students who need Tier Two interventions, these partnerships should be homogeneous and the teacher should check in with these groups to ensure that data is entered accurately.

Tier Three: One on One

Students will work one on one with a teacher to ensure that data collection is accurate.

Tier One: Whole Group (Scatter Plot Creation)

1. Display examples of scatter plot graphs throughout the room.

2. Ask students to make observations about each graph using sticky notes.

3. Share observations and build a definition of a scatter plot based on what students observed.

4. Explain that scatter plots are similar to line graphs.

5. A scatter plot has an x- and a y-axis. Each dot on a scatter plot represents a piece of data. In this case, the dots represent temperature and absences.

6. Scatter plots illustrate a correlation, or relationship, between data.

7. Create an x- and a y-axis on the chart.

8. Identify the x-axis as the daily temperature and the y-axis as number of absences.

9. Label appropriately.

10. Take the Day One temperature and number of absences and plot them on the graph by marking a dot that lines up with the temperature on the x-axis and the number of absences on the y-axis. Prominently display this model scatter plot. Possible tools to use are a magnetic whiteboard or a felt board with Velcro counters.

11. Students use graph paper to create a scatter plot.

Tier Two: Partner Activity (May Also Be Used at Tier One)

1. After whole group modeling, students who need Tier Two Interventions are put into mixed-ability partnerships.

2. Partners receive coaching from the teacher.
   a. review of x- and y-axes
   b. organization of data on the x- and y-axes
   c. accuracy in plotting data

Tier Three: One on One

- Students receive one-on-one instruction from the teacher using additional tools and support. For example, use overhead transparency paper and dry erase markers to create a scatter plot.
- Make available the x- and y-axes with titles already created so the student only has to plot the information. The student uses the same x- and y-axes that the teacher used during whole class modeling and fills in the existing data. The student may use paper counters or magnets to manipulate the data.

Tier One: Whole Group (Scatter Plot Analysis)

1. Once all the data has been recorded, refer back to the class scatter plot. Complete this on your own or with one of your students who need Tier Three interventions as suggested above.

2. Make general observations and ask students to do the same. Encourage students to talk in pairs or groups and examine their own graphs.

   a. What do you notice about the data?
   b. How is it organized?
   c. Is there a pattern?

3. Explain that there are four types of correlations. Each can be determined by "eyeballing" the graph or, more accurately, constructing the line of best fit. A line of best fit is a line that represents the data trend. Several ways to construct best-fit lines can be found online.

   a. Positive: A positive correlation exists when the y-value increases as the x-value increases. The line of best fit has a positive, or upward, slope (see Figure 6.4).
   b. Negative: A scatter plot shows a negative correlation when the y-value decreases as the x-value increases. The line of best fit has a negative, or downward, slope (see Figure 6.5 on page 118).
   c. Strong: A strong correlation exists when a majority of the data lies close to the line of best fit (see Figure 6.6 on page 118).
   d. Weak: A weak correlation exists when a majority of the data lies further away from the line of best fit (Figure 6.7 on page 118).

4. Note to students: Correlations can be weak negative, strong negative, weak positive, or strong positive.

5. Print out real examples of scatter plots (which can easily be found online) and determine what type of correlation the graph depicts.

Figure 6.4   Temperature Graph: Positive Correlation

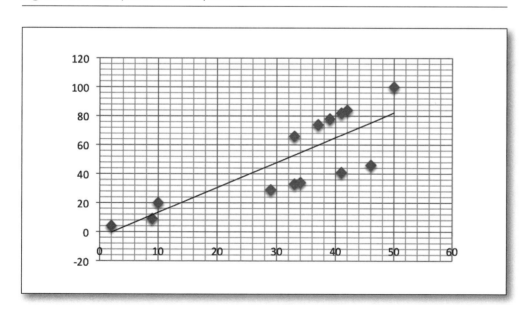

Figure 6.5 Temperature Graph: Negative Correlation

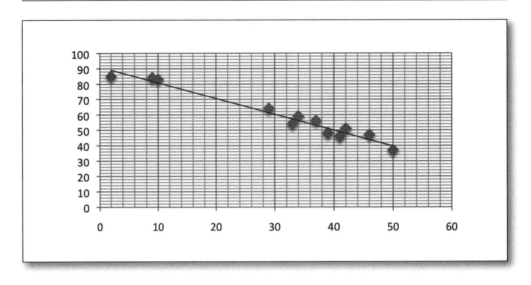

Figure 6.6 Temperature Graph: Strong Correlation

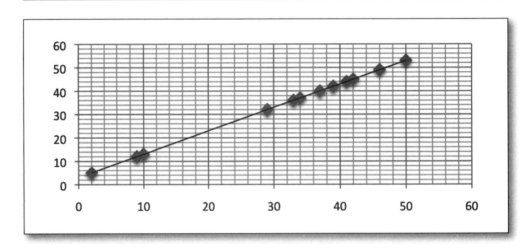

Figure 6.7 Temperature Graph: Weak Correlation

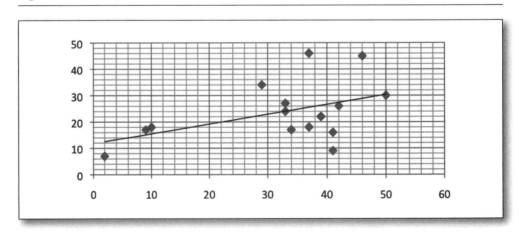

6. Think aloud to explicitly model how you determine the type of correlation for each example.

7. Tell students to analyze the scatter plot they created and determine the type of correlation.

8. Have students provide a written explanation of the correlations. Pair students who are weak in written expression but strong in math understanding with partners who have the skill to model how the explanation should be written.

Tier Two: Partner Activity (May Also Be Used at Tier One)

1. Students work in the same partnerships as for the previous steps and use counters to create a model of the four types of correlations.
   a. Give students time to work in groups to create each model and identify the correlations.
   b. Provide support to groups as necessary.

2. Students use models they just created to determine the type of correlation for the data on their scatter plot.

3. The teacher monitors partners and can provide students with copies of the scatter plots from the lesson for an additional visual aid.

Tier Three: One on One

Students work one on one with the teacher to determine the type of correlation displayed on the scatter plot. Students should have all visual aids and models for reference.

Manipulatives Center

Students work in tiered groups (Tier One is mixed levels, Tier Two is same ability with some peer or teacher support, and Tier Three is one-on-one instruction) to create and analyze scatter plot graphs using a variety of materials. Provide data for students to graph (education levels and income, for example) and a variety of materials such as

- counters;
- card stock (for the graph);
- dry erase boards and markers;
- construction paper;
- buttons;
- cellophane (to make overlays for the graphs);
- index cards for identifying the type of correlation; and
- a pegboard (available at any home supply store) and pegs.

Students work collaboratively to plan and create a scatter plot based on the data provided or student-generated data.

1. Students discuss the type of correlation the data shows.

2. Students write an explanation of their findings.

Extension Activities Center

Students will use their manila folder and graph paper for a variety of other activities, including

- using another type of graph (histogram, line graph, or stem/leaf plot) to analyze the same data from this lesson;
- continuing to record temperature and absences across a longer period of time, then reanalyzing the correlation between the two; and
- asking the school for permission to use two weeks' worth of attendance records from previous years and research the daily temperatures for that time period. Collect data for a two-week period from each season and use a scatter plot to display the correlation between absence rates and the seasons. Students can also make predictions about how or if the correlation between seasons is positive, negative, weak, or strong.

To Differentiate

- Differentiate by number of days in data, manipulatives, support, and grouping.
- Provide small group or individual coaching with a teacher, intervention specialist, or peer tutor.

English as a Second Language and English Language Learners

1. Explicitly teach vocabulary and have words displayed prominently in an organized manner (word wall) in the classroom for easy review. Such vocabulary words include

   a. *x- and y-axes;*
   b. *plot;*
   c. *scatter;*
   d. *data;*
   e. *line of best fit;*
   f. *analysis;*
   g. *correlation;*
   h. *positive;*
   i. *negative;*
   j. *weak;* and
   k. *strong.*

2. Include a physical object or picture next to each vocabulary word that represents that word that you are teaching.

3. Students may also want to keep a personal vocabulary list for easy reference.

4. Play a vocabulary game to aid in memorization of words.

Assessment

Students will complete their own scatter plots using a variety of tools such as graph paper, three-dimensional models with manipulatives (magnets, buttons, pegs, or the like), or technology (graphing or spreadsheet software, graphing websites). Students will provide a written explanation of the correlation between absences and temperature.

Rubric: Creating and Analyzing a Scatter Plot Graph

Category	1	2	3	4
Students will use a variety of tools to create a scatter plot graph to display data collected.	Students need extensive teacher support to create a scatter plot graph.	Students need some teacher support to create a scatter plot graph.	Students need little teacher support in using manipulatives to create a scatter plot chart.	Students independently create a scatter plot graph using manipulatives.
Students will analyze the scatter plot graph to determine the type of correlation between daily temperature and student absences.	Students identify one correlation between temperature and absences with extensive teacher support.	Students make two correlations between temperature and absences with some teacher support.	Students make one correlation between temperature and absences without teacher support.	Students make two correlations between temperature and absences without teacher support.

Across the Curriculum

Whether in social studies, science, or math, teachers can use this approach to help students understand the relationships between

- rates of disease and distance to a source of drinking water;
- body weight and heart disease;
- rate of alcoholism and income; or
- number of calories and grams of fat in their favorite foods.

MATH VOCABULARY ■

The lesson plan samples and strategy examples in the chapter focused on vocabulary provide excellent examples for how to reinforce math vocabulary. Rather than create a separate lesson plan for math vocabulary, I'd like to share an example I saw effectively demonstrated at Permian High School in Odessa, Texas.

Danna McAnnelly and Brandi Pettus, co-teachers at the 10th-grade level, made vocabulary review part of their teaching practice. One of the techniques they used was to choose a state test question and spend five minutes a class period, usually at the end of class, reviewing the vocabulary in that item. They did not spend any time working out the math. They only focused on the vocabulary.

They presented a test question via laptop and projector on a screen. All students had an index card. They were to review the question presented and list any words that they did not understand on that index card. Given that the class had a large bilingual population, this was an especially important exercise. The teachers collected the index cards as the students finished. They then used the information on the cards to drive vocabulary instruction throughout the semester.

In addition to having students list the words on an index card, they discussed the question with the class as a whole. I was fascinated to learn that the students found the question phrase, "Which of the following best represents . . ." the most challenging part of the test item. We tend to focus on math skills in preparation for state tests in math; however, we also need to concentrate on vocabulary. Many students may do poorly on the test because of a lack of vocabulary understanding rather than a lack of math skill.

It's important to teach math vocabulary to all students. It's critical for nonresponders.

Also, teach students to look for clue words in math word problems.

- Clue words for addition: *sum, total, in all, perimeter*
- Clue words for subtraction: *difference, how much more, exceed*
- Clue words for multiplication: *product, total, area, times*
- Clue words for division: *share, distribute, quotient, average*

■ DECLUTTER THE MATH

From *Memorization and Test Taking Strategies for the Differentiated, Inclusive and RTI Classroom*, Susan Gingras Fitzell, 2010.

Particularly in learning math, disorganized workspaces clutter up working memory because students are too busy trying to make order out of chaos to focus on the actual math problem. Helping students organize their workspace is one of the best ways we can help students with math (Levine, 2003). Following are some simple solutions to organizing math instruction for students.

- Write down the steps to the problem before solving it.
- Avoid mental arithmetic; use a scratch pad or scrap paper.
- Use graph or lined paper to complete math problems:
  o Give your students grid paper or have them turn their lined paper sideways (see Figure 6.8).
  o Fold their lined paper into squares and do one problem in each square.
- Have students work their problems by lining the numbers up in the columns.
- When testing or doing math handouts on plain paper, put a piece of dark lined paper or grid paper under the math page. Students will be able to see the lines through the page and will keep their math organized.
- If they become overwhelmed by looking at the entire test page, have students use blank paper to cover up everything but the problem they are working on so they don't become stressed. When they do not have to look at everything at once, they can focus more productively.

When students are working to organize their workspace or trying to decipher their work, they are using up working memory on organization rather than the math process. These strategies allow them to focus on the math.

Figure 6.8 Grid Paper

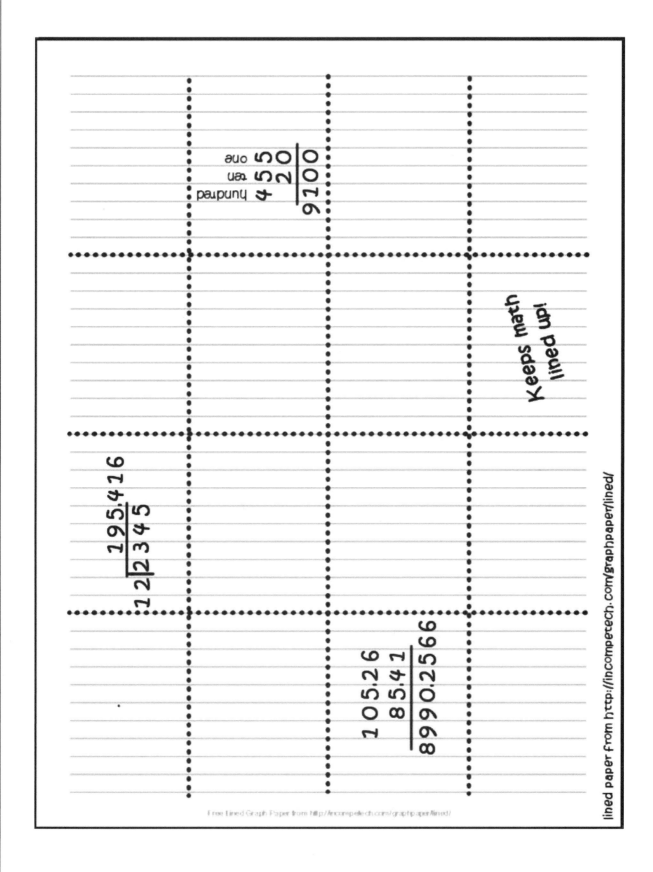

7

Cross-Curricular Interventions for Higher-Order Thinking and Recall

■ MIND MAPPING, GRAPHIC ROADMAPS, AND VISUAL ORGANIZERS

I started using mind mapping after reading *I Can See You Naked: A Fearless Guide to Making Great Presentations* by Ron Hoff (1988). My first presentation was drawn out like a colorful board game with a route to follow, arrows, and picture images of what I was going to do. I remember thinking how much easier it was to use than index cards with a script written on them. It was also much less restricting. I did not feel tied to reading the cards. Rather, I looked at the picture and went from memory. It saved me from the plight of many presenters, that of being tied to a script.

The technique worked so well for me that I started expanding the idea into my teaching efforts. As I read selections from English texts to my students, I drew the events out on paper in map and graphic format. I would often interject silly ditties and exclamations of passion in an effort to make what I was reading to them stick out in their memories. Given that my students were in their "cool" teenage years, they would often look at me and say, "You are crazy!" My pat answer was always, "Yes, I am, but you'll remember this because of it." Moreover, they did.

Students learn and remember mind maps better if they create them out of their own mental images and patterns. As a parent who has spent my children's lifetimes trying to teach them how to learn, I was very excited when I walked into my daughter Shivahn's college apartment and found mind maps, mnemonics, color, and the like all over one of her walls. Now, it's not unusual to find mandalas on her door or on her walls, or flash cards scattered about, but this was a huge mind map made from recycled 8.5-by-11-inch sheets of paper (see Figure 7.1). I had no idea what it all meant, but I do know it helped her to get an A in the course. My daughter cowrote a book with me, *Umm . . . Studying? What's That?*, so it's reassuring to know that she didn't just write the book but also used the strategies and shared them with her peers.

Figure 7.1 Engineering Student's Dorm Room Mind Map Wall

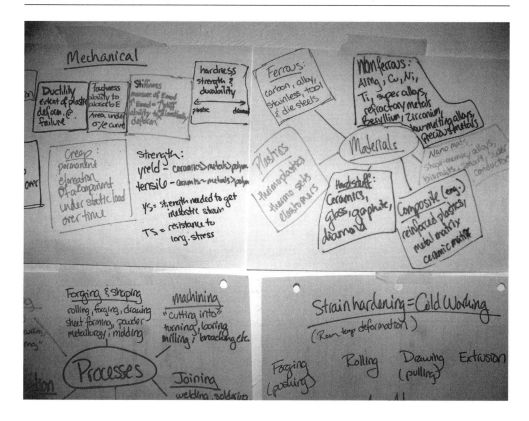

Research Background

Developing cognitive maps and using advance organizers increase critical thinking skills (Barba & Merchant, 1990; Snapp & Glover, 1990; Tierney, Soter, O'Flavahan, & McGinley, 1989).

Long-term memory files information in the brain through patterns, procedures, categories, pairs, and rules. A mind map uses at least three of these five ways to store information. A classic mind map begins with a word, phrase, or idea, typically placed in the center of a sheet of paper. As the author of the mind map expands upon the word or phrase in the middle, the mind map expands to include various ideas that come to mind when considering that center prompt.

Mind maps enable the brain to categorize information. A mind map is a nonlinguistic representation method of organizing information that enables students to file information away in long-term memory in multiple modes or memory packets.

Learning Objectives

- To improve recall of information presented
- To incorporate multiple modes of storing information in long-term memory so that all types of learners can be successful
- To create meaningful connections between previously learned information, new information, and connected information
- To categorize, create paired associations, and incorporate nonlinguistic representation and critical thinking skills into the learning process

Addresses These Nonresponder Indicators

- There are deficits in recoding incoming information into meaningful connections.
- The student demonstrates minimal higher-order thinking, such as problem solving, sequencing, and organizing thoughts into a meaningful pattern.
- The student has difficulty activating prior knowledge and retrieving information learned.
- The student has difficulty remembering what the teacher says in class.
- The student has difficulty seeing patterns in math problems.
- The student has difficulty writing a paragraph or essay.
- The student has poor auditory short-term memory.
- The student has problems categorizing information, pairing information, and formulating associations when reading or writing.
- The student struggles with focusing, planning, and organizing.

Materials Needed

- Chart paper and crayons or markers; copy paper and colored pencils, markers, and gel pens
- Sample mind maps on another topic to provide a model or example
- Textbook, literature, class notes, or other source of content to be mind mapped

Approximate Time Frame for Completion

This lesson plan may take more than one class period, depending on class length.

- Whole group strategy (creating the mind map): 10 to 15 minutes

> *Note:* Students may need more time. Check in with each group about 10 minutes into the activity to ensure that all groups are working to potential and are remaining on task.

- Resulting discussion or extension learning: variable
- Tier Two and Tier Three activities: 15 minutes or less, depending on available time
- Extension activities: variable

Intervention Procedure and Scripts

Tier One/Small Group

1. First, explain what a mind map is (see Figure 7.2).

Figure 7.2   Social Studies Mind Map

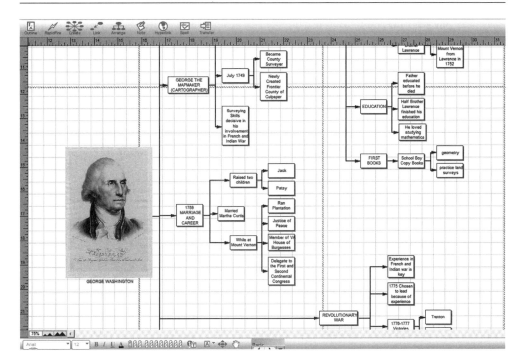

2. Put students in mixed-ability groups of two or three. Use the High with Middle, Middle with Low grouping strategy (see Figure 2.5 on page 18). Give each group paper for making a chart.

3. Give each student a different color marker, pencil, or crayon.

4. Students put their names on the paper in their color.

> *Note to high school teachers:* I used to be reluctant to use crayons with Grades 9 through 12 until faced with a tight budget. Crayons work just fine and can be a lesson in frugality for students. Simply state the realities of your budget. If they want to bring in their own markers, they can. Otherwise, if all you can afford is crayons, they work just fine.

5. Ask students
   a. to contribute words that come to mind when they think of (the topic to be written about); and
   b. what images come to mind when they think about (the topic).

6. Tell students to list their ideas on the topic using the mind map format to create logical connections. *Important:* Students take turns listing their words in the mind map by passing the paper around the table. They list their words in their color.

7. Enhance the mind map with stick figure images, color, and meaningful symbols.

Tier Two and Three: One on One

1. Ask students
   a. to contribute words that come to mind when they think of <u>(the topic to be written about)</u>; and
   b. what images come to mind when they think about <u>(the topic)</u>.

2. Tell students to list their ideas on the topic using the mind map format to create logical connections.

3. Enhance the mind map with stick figure images, color, and meaningful symbols.

Tier Two and Three: One on One

1. Ask students
   a. to pull key words from the reading: events, characters, dates tied to something meaningful (list both together), places, cause and effect, etc.; and
   b. what images come to mind when they think about these key words.

2. Tell students to list their ideas on the topic using the mind map format to create logical connections.

3. Enhance the mind map with stick figure images, color, and meaningful symbols.

Extension: Making More of the Mind Map

Students can illustrate the ideas on their mind map by placing photographs, illustrations, and links to relevant websites. For example, they can

- Take photographs to illustrate their ideas using the digital camera and upload them
- Scan photographs and pictures out of books and magazines
- Copy quotes relevant to the topic from literature, magazines, or newspapers
- Write up quotes from the class discussion

Note: When students make spelling errors at this phase of the creative process, note the errors but let them go. Correcting spelling while students are creating will cause them to clutter their working memory with rules and not allow enough space for coming up with ideas.

Application Example: Writing in the Content Area (Social Studies)

A student created a social studies mind map (see Figure 7.2 on page 127) as the outline of his paper and presentation on George Washington's life and accomplishments.

Application Example: Independent Reading in the Content Area (Science)

Figure 7.3 is a graphic representation of the life history of stars. This representation visually explains the process, whereas a linear outline does not convey that process with the same clarity.

Figure 7.3   Science Mind Map

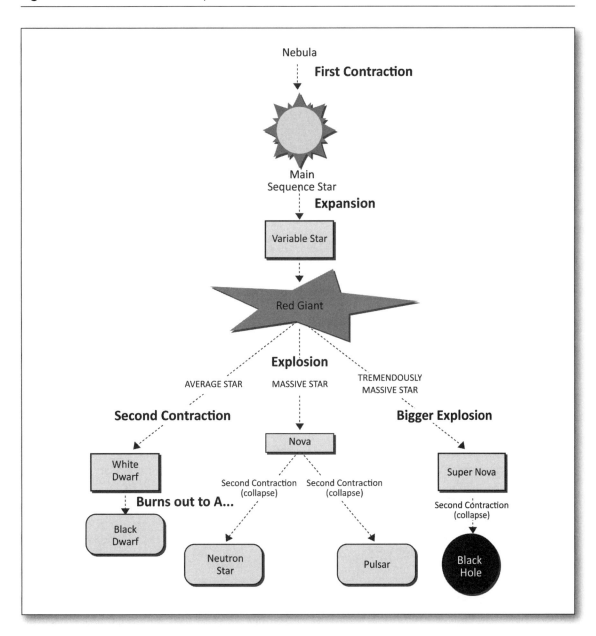

Assessment

Mind Map Rubric

Category	1	2	3	4
Neatness and Presentation	The mind map is not neat enough to understand.	The mind map is not neat enough to understand most concepts.	The mind map is well presented and most of the information is easy to understand.	The mind map is well presented and all the information is easy to understand.
Use of Images and Symbols	The mind map includes few images.	The mind map includes some images.	Some categories are enhanced with simple symbols or diagrams.	Most categories are enhanced with simple symbols or diagrams.
Use of Color	The mind map lacks color.	Uses color, but not to categorize throughout the mind map.	Color demonstrates some connections or topics throughout the mind map.	Uses color to show all connections or to categorize topics throughout the mind map.
Understanding	The mind map includes two or fewer elements for each category.	The mind map includes at least two elements demonstrating comprehension for some categories.	The mind map contains three elements for some categories.	The mind map contains at least three elements for each category.

■ STRATEGY TO REMEMBER SEQUENCES

Many years before I had any research on sequencing as an intervention strategy, I discovered a striking correlation between the cognitive test data for specific students on sequencing subtests and their ability to answer cause-and-effect questions, retell a story, or remember a timeline in history. Students with low scores on sequencing subtests generally did poorly on academic tasks that required the ability to sequence. That should not be surprising; however, prior to that moment of realization, I had not made the connection between the data and the student outcomes.

One day, I sat with my co-teacher and reviewed the cognitive testing scores of one of the students we both taught. As we reviewed the test results and considered the child, we both gained a deeper understanding of that student's challenges as well as of ways to address his needs. The following is one of the strategies we incorporated into our teaching.

Research Background

Some students struggle to remember sequences. They cannot remember a timeline in history, the storyline in a short story, the steps to solve a geometric proof, or the sequence of a cycle in science (Levine, 2003). How might we support students in recalling sequences? One approach is to make the sequence visually concrete.

Learning Objectives

- To provide a recall strategy incorporating graphics created by the student in a specific, sequential fashion
- To improve recall of data for which proper sequencing is required
- To incorporate multiple modes of storing information in long-term memory, so that all types of learners can be successful
- To create meaningful connections between new information and visual cues (nonlinguistic representation) to enable students to remember sequential information in the correct order
- To categorize, create paired associations, and incorporate nonlinguistic representation and critical thinking skills into the learning process

Addresses These Nonresponder Indicators

- The student has difficulty focusing, planning, and organizing.
- The student has difficulty remembering timelines; cycles in science; or the steps for solving a math problem, researching a hypothesis, or any given task.
- The student has difficulty remembering what the teacher says in class.
- The student has difficulty retrieving information learned in the correct sequence.
- The student has difficulty with higher-order thinking such as problem solving, sequencing, and organizing thoughts into a meaningful pattern.
- The student is unable to recode incoming information into meaningful connections.
- The student is unable to arrange information to use it effectively.
- The student has poor auditory short-term memory.

Materials Needed

- Adding machine or cash register tape
- Colored pencils, markers, or gel pens
- Sample sequence strips on another topic to provide a model or example
- Textbook, literature, class notes, or other source of content to be sequenced

Approximate Time Frame for Completion

- Main whole group activity (Introduction to Sequence Strip Mapping): 15 to 30 minutes, depending on your objectives
- Partner work: 10 to 15 minutes
- Independent practice and peer feedback: 10 to 15 minutes

Intervention Procedure and Scripts

Explain what a sequence strip is (see Figure 7.4).

Figure 7.4 Sequence Strip Example

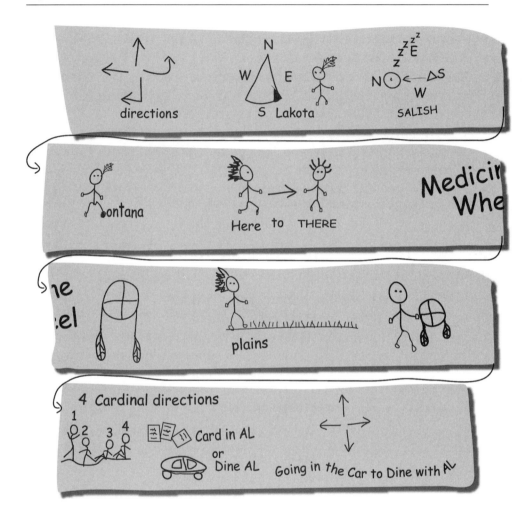

*Tier One/Whole Class: Introduction
to Sequence Strip Mapping*

1. Give students an adding machine or cash register tape.

2. Choose text, note, timeline, or process that students will be sequencing.

3. Provide instruction (read aloud, review notes, present new information, etc.) to students. When a key fact, event, cause-and-effect relationship, vocabulary word, or date is presented, *stop*.

4. Tell students to take their writing utensils and paper tape in hand. Ask them what was important in what you just presented or read.

5. Verify that they have identified the correct information, and then summarize it into a key word that will become the label for that information on the paper tape.

6. Draw a stick figure representation of that information on the board. Students should copy the teacher's drawing on their paper strip (or they may create their own image; what is critical is that the image is meaningful to the student).

7. Students should have a picture with a label (see Figure 7.5).

8. Continue this process until students have a completed sequence strip highlighting the most important concepts, connections, and cause-and-effect relations outlined on their paper tape.

Figure 7.5

The Four Directions

Native Americans use directions in many aspects of their lives. The Lakota (luh-KO-tuh), a tribe from the Great Plains, set up their teepees so that they faced the east. There were tribes like the Salish (SAY-lish) that slept by laying their heads to the north. Because Native Americans traveled the plains, directions were a very important part of their culture.

MEDICINE WHEELS

Circles play a great role in the culture of the American Northwest . The **medicine wheel** was a circle in the Native American culture that had particular significance. The medicine wheel is a spiritual symbol to the plains tribes.

*Tier One/Whole Class: Sequence Strip
Mapping Variation (Time-Saver)*

After students become familiar with the technique and competent in using the strategy independently, advance to the following options.

Option One

1. While providing instruction in class, repeat Steps 1 through 8 above. However, only write down the key word or phrase (label). Essentially, they are doing Step 6 at home. They label in class and illustrate for homework.

2. Have students draw a picture for each label for homework or independent practice. This ensures that they will have to revisit the information again. Do not allow too much time between the verbal component and the drawing component. Ideally, students will draw pictures approximately three to six hours later. This gap in time is the first step to moving the information from short-term memory to working memory.

Option Two

1. Students work independently or in pairs.

2. As students are reading a textbook or story, instruct them to draw pictures on adding machine tape of the important information (characters, historical figures, places, events, etc.) in the order that they appear in the information source. Walk students through the process.

   a. Remind students to start at the beginning of the tape and work left to right.
   b. Have models available as visual reminders for students.

Application Example

Social Studies (See Figures 7.4 and 7.5 Shown Previously)

While your students read about how the Lakota used directions for navigation, they draw a picture of the key points on the tape.

The chapter proceeds to describe types of information recorded by Native Americans, such as the position of the sun and the moon, neighboring sites, etc.

Students draw and label that information in the same sequence that the textbook lists or describes it. See the example shown previously (Figure 7.4).

When complete, the student has a timeline or storyline, in sequential order, of the events in the textbook or story. This visual memory tool will help them to remember the information in the order that it happened.

Assessment

Sequencing Rubric

Category	1	2	3	4
Neatness and Presentation	Is not neat enough to understand.	Presents well; some of the information is difficult to understand.	Most of the information is easy to understand.	All the information is easy to understand.
Use of Images and Symbols	The sequence strip includes some images.	Enhances a few labels with simple symbols or diagrams.	Enhances some labels with simple symbols or diagrams.	Enhances most labels with simple symbols or diagrams.
Use of Color	The sequence strip lacks color.	Uses colors, but does not categorize or chunk information with colors.	Uses color to demonstrate some connections or topics throughout the sequence strip.	Uses color to show all connections or to categorize topics throughout the sequence strip.
Includes Major Events	Excludes many major events, and includes too many trivial events.	Includes some trivial events while major events are missing.	Includes most of the important or interesting events, but only one or two major events.	Includes important and interesting events without excluding any major details.

ADDITIONAL NONLINGUISTIC INTERVENTIONS: GRAPHIC NOTES

A highly effective way to introduce a new concept or topic to students is to utilize the pictures in the textbook, or to find related pictures and provide students with the opportunity to

- Predict what might be happening in the picture
- Observe details in the picture as a crime scene investigator (CSI) might as a precursor to learning the facts
- Analyze a picture for political themes, key events, social values, etc.
- Simply figure out the *Who, What, When, Where,* and *Why* of the visual on their own before being taught the material

These graphic notes are effective for all three tiers as well as whole class, small group, or one on one activities. See Figures 7.6 and 7.7 for examples.

Figure 7.6 Graphic Notes, Example 1

Image from iStockphoto.com. Text by Catherine Laplace.

Figure 7.7 Graphic Notes, Example 2

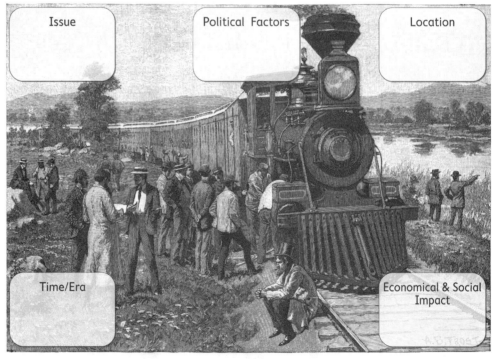

Image from iStockphoto.com. Text by Catherine Laplace.

GROUP AND CLASSIFY INFORMATION ■ TO ENHANCE LONG-TERM MEMORY

Essentially, this sample lesson plan models grouping and classifying by using mind maps in a lesson plan focused on teaching students to identify genre in literature. I call this *layering techniques* to get the most out of available class time.

I chose genre specifically because it is familiar to teachers and is an educational standard. What is not dictated in our state standards, however, is how we go about teaching genre. Consequently, the reader may gain some additional ideas for presentation as well as a sampleof how it may be adjusted for different student levels in the differentiated classroom.

Research Background

Mind maps complement the way the brain naturally categorizes information. The schema, or mental structure, of the mind contains all of our preexisting knowledge sorted into themes. As the mind takes in new information, it matches it with an already familiar theme in order to make sense of it.

The use of mind maps in the classroom provides students with a visual way to categorize data that will in turn make new information easier for students to comprehend. It also increases their ability to recall the information later. (Ausubel, 1963; Hyerle, 2009; Marzano et al., 2001; Moore & Readence, 1984).

Learning Objectives

- To organize information according to a theme
- To discover how subthemes are interrelated
- To analyze information and summarize it while leaving out extraneous information
- To use appropriate vocabulary in describing the features observed

Addresses These Nonresponder Indicators

- The student has Attention Deficit Disorder.
- The student has an auditory learning deficit.
- The student has difficulty activating prior knowledge and retrieving information learned.
- The student has difficulty recoding incoming information into meaningful information.
- The student has difficulty remembering what the teacher says in class.
- The student has difficulty with higher-order thinking such as problem solving and comparing and contrasting.
- The student has notetaking deficiencies, specifically, with grouping and classifying pertinent information.

Materials Needed

- Literature books of various genres
- Genre information
- Rubric
- Group segment of the mind map and blank individual mind maps
- Colored pencils, pens, or markers for each group

Approximate Time Frame for Completion

This lesson plan may take more than one class period, depending on class length.

- Main whole group activities: 10 to 15 minutes
- Small group practice and interventions: 15 to 30 minutes (variable, depending on class dynamics and student participation)
- Extension learning: variable

Intervention Procedure and Scripts

Part One: Tier One/Whole Group

1. Draw a mind map on the board and write the word *genre* along with its definition in the middle of it: *A genre is a category of literary composition characterized by a particular style, form, or content.*

   Examples of genre are *allegory, comedy, creative nonfiction, epic, essay, lyric, motion picture scenario, novel, pastoral, satire, short story, television play, tragedy, poetry, science fiction, fantasy, fairy tales, tall tales, folk tales, myths and legends, historical fiction, mystery, nonfiction, biography,* and *autobiography.*

2. Discuss genre with the students.

Part Two: Tier One/Tier Two/Small Groups

> *Note:* Students who need Tier Two support gain those supports in mixed-ability groups with close supervision by the teacher or an intervention specialist. Peer tutoring is a research-based practice and, when done under the close guidance of teachers and intervention specialists, can be used to provide Tier Two interventions.

1. Place students in preselected small groups (three to five students), ensuring a mixture of ability levels.

2. Hand out an assortment of literature books, children's books representing a variety of reading levels and sophistication, or short stories to each small group.

3. Ask students to look through their group's books and use a list of genres to classify the books.

4. They may create their own classifications or include some not on the list.

5. If they create their own, they must explain the rationale behind the genre.

Part Three: Tier One/Whole Group

1. Once the small groups have compiled their list, discuss each group's findings as a class.

2. Guide a discussion.

3. Ask each group to share a genre they identified and record it on the board as part of the mind map started in Part One.

4. Continue until an adequate number of genres have been identified and listed.

5. Choose one genre as an example.

6. Create extensions to that section of the mind map.

7. With the class, add literary examples of that classification to the mind map.

8. Use a different color for each section to help students visualize the classifications.

Extension

Students may compare and contrast two similar genres using the Compare and Contrast Genre Map (see Figure 7.8 on page 140). Examples of genres that could be compared include science fiction and fantasy; myths and legends, and tall tales; biography and autobiography; and fairy tales and folk tales.

To Differentiate

- Provide a typed copy of the completed mind map to students who have difficulty taking notes.
- Have students choose their own literature for a genre exercise from a wide range of reading levels.
- Have students create a human mind map with each student holding a sheet of paper with their piece of the map. For example, one student stands in the middle of a group and holds the name of the genre. That center student holds several long strands of string. Other students take the end of the string and hold a sheet of paper that lists the characteristics of that genre, etc.
- Offer students a choice between creating a poster-sized mind map or a three-dimensional mobile mind map.

Across the Curriculum

A Compare and Contrast Genre Map is simply a graphic organizer that is being implemented for the specific content goal of understanding genre through grouping and classifying. However, mind maps can be used any time students need to cover a large amount of material quickly.

- After introducing the lesson objective for a unit of study, give each group a piece of the unit to investigate. As they research, they record information in the mind map. As each group presents its data to the class, the others will add the information to their mind maps.

- A mind map can also be used to introduce a new unit or theme and then be added to as new information or definitions are introduced to the class. Give students a blank copy of the mind map that they can fill in and keep for studying.

This provides a great way to review daily and connect all the material in a logical way. Encourage students to use their mind maps to study before a test. Mind maps are more efficient than traditional notes because when students study they are able to see the whole concept and how everything connects. Use of mind maps also teaches to a variety of learning preferences at the same time.

- Social studies teachers can use this approach to organize a specific theme as it applies to different time periods or social groups. Examples might include technology and its effects on the family unit, the doctrine of nonviolence and how it has influenced social change, or transportation and how it has encouraged globalization.

Figure 7.8   Compare and Contrast Genre Map

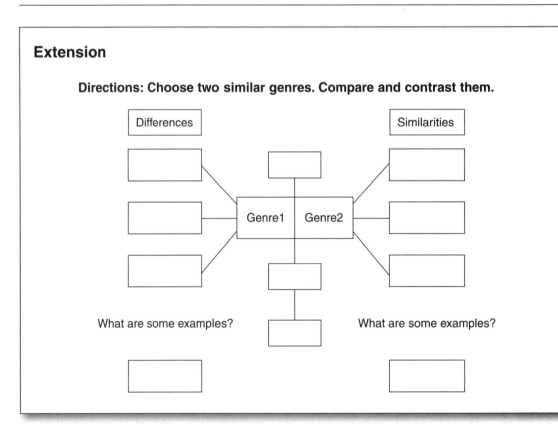

Extension

Directions: Choose two similar genres. Compare and contrast them.

Differences

Similarities

Genre1   Genre2

What are some examples?

What are some examples?

- Science teachers can use this strategy to connect new definitions to a central theme. Examples might include the periodic table and the element groups and families, habitats and their characteristics, or the human body and its systems.
- Math teachers might apply this to areas such as geometry and proofs, algebra and types of equations, or trigonometry and angles.
- In all subject areas, teachers may apply classification and grouping in a variety of ways in addition to those presented.
- For independent writing assignments, have students write a short story, play, or short comic book that applies to the area of study.
- For independent reading, students select books or articles on the subject area and build a mind map covering the characteristics being studied.

Assessment

Mind Map Rubric

Category	1	2	3	4
Neatness and Presentation	Writes illegibly. Misspells genre-related words. Writes multiple sections in one color.	Prepares a messy presentation. Misspells three to four genre-related words. Writes each section in a different color.	Prepares a neat and orderly presentation overall. Spells genre-related words correctly.	Prepares an exceptionally neat and orderly presentation.
Content	The mind map does not demonstrate student understanding of the mapped topic.	The mind map misses most of the major components of the mapped topic.	The mind map misses some major components of the mapped topic.	The mind map includes the major components of the mapped topic.
Color	The mind map is not colored.	The student does not use color to chunk the branches and categories in the map. Color is decorative rather than meaningful.	The student uses color to chunk the branches and categories. Yet chunks are not always clearly designated.	The student uses color to chunk the branches and categories in a meaningful way. Each branch and category is clearly differentiated by color.
Verbosity	The mind map presents only one word or term on each branch.	The mind map presents multiple words or terms on some of the branches. Many branches appear incomplete.	The mind map presents multiple words or terms on many of the branches. Some branches appear incomplete.	The mind map presents multiple words or terms on most or all of the branches.

■ ANALOGIES

My experiences over many years in the trenches as a classroom teacher have repeatedly reinforced the value of analogies as a teaching and learning tool. Analogies that are drawn from student experience and that can be connected to new information have been more successful in getting a point across or fostering memorization than almost any other method.

The science analogy included in this sample lesson plan came from my co-teaching and inclusion experience. My co-teacher and I would alternate introducing the units. When it was my turn to introduce the respiratory system, I struggled to help students find a way to understand parts of the body that they could not physically see. The ceramic models we had available to us were lacking, to say the least, and did not connect to understandings that students already had in place.

I will admit that it took time to find physical objects to represent all the parts of the respiratory system; however, I found it an entertaining challenge—a game, in a sense. The morning that I was introducing the lesson, I showed up to class with two pillowcases filled with my analogous objects. As I dumped the items on the table, my co-teacher looked at me in confusion and surprise. I explained my plan and laid the objects out in the same order they would be used as air passed through the body. When the time came for me to share this experiment with the students, I gathered them around the table and explained my process. I will admit that, given these were 10th graders and unused to such methods, I got some rolled eyes and teasing about what I had done. Undaunted, I began the lesson.

As I proceeded, I saw understanding reflected in the students' eyes and heard it in their responses. "What would happen to a vacuum cleaner hose when I turned on the vacuum if there were no metal rings to hold it open?" "It would collapse and stick together. No air would be able to get through," one student answered. Others agreed and grasped the concept. "OK," I explained, "Just like the vacuum cleaner hose has metal rings to keep it open as air passes through, the trachea has cartilage rings to keep it open when we breathe so that air can pass through."

I could see it start to click with the students. The analogy worked. If you don't have time to find objects to represent concepts you are teaching, assign it for homework. Let students create the analogies. The only time I would not suggest this is if you are studying the reproductive system.

Research Background

When people use analogies to learn a new topic or solve a problem, they have a higher success rate because they make connections between new knowledge and familiar ideas or models (schema). When three groups of people were asked to solve a medical problem, 75% of the group that was told to use an analogy to solve the problem were successful (Gick & Holyoak, 1983, p. 4). Analogies prove to be a useful tool in the classroom. Rule and Furletti (2004) found that form and analogy boxes improved student performance when learning about different body systems. Analogy boxes contain objects and cards that demonstrate similarities between the new concept (for example, the eye of the nervous system) and the analogy (a camera lens).

Students will enjoy higher levels of success when they are very familiar with the analogies used. In one study, Friedel, Gabel, and Samuel found that teachers often used analogies that related to their own experience and, as a result, students failed to understand the relationships between the new concept and analogy (Rule & Furletti, 2004). Teachers must choose analogies that their students will understand and must also emphasize the limits of the analogy to prevent student misconception.

Learning Objectives

- To enhance long-term memory (recall and recognition)
- To make connections between the known and unknown
- To increase comprehension by relating concrete representation with new abstract concepts

Addresses These Nonresponder Indicators

- The student needs to develop the automaticity of skills (for example, memorizing multiplication tables or spelling of certain words so they are automatic).
- The student has difficulty processing information in a way that is personally meaningful.
- The student does not activate prior knowledge (has difficulty retrieving information learned).
- The student comprehends new and abstract concepts poorly.
- The student has long-term memory deficits.
- The student has problems relating and applying new information.
- The student struggles with recall and recognition.
- The student has trouble remembering what the teacher says in class.
- The student is unable to connect new information with previous knowledge.
- The student is unable to recode incoming information into meaningful learning.

Materials Needed

Create a description of the new concept you are about to teach. It might be a process such as how a bill becomes a law, a historical event such as the Cold War or the French Revolution, or a person like the President of the United States. Students should have read the description before beginning the lesson (see Figure 7.9).

Figure 7.9 Cold War Map

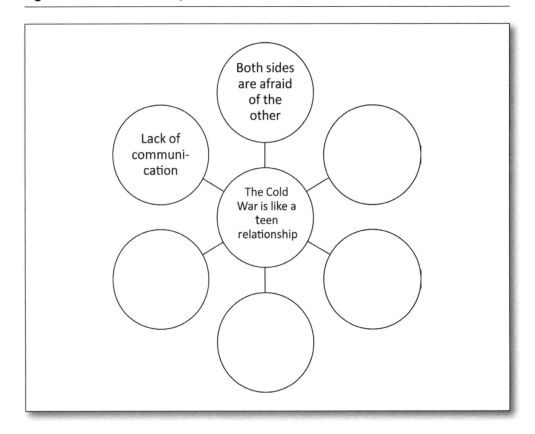

Approximate Time Frame for Completion

This lesson plan may take more than one class period, depending on class length.

- Whole group strategy (brainstorming the analogy): 10 to 20 minutes
- Small group practice: 10 to 15 minutes (variable, depending on class dynamics and student participation)
- Resulting discussion and creating visual and written representations of analogy: variable

Intervention Procedure and Scripts

Tier One: Whole Class

1. Either in small groups or at the board, students generate a list of adjectives or steps to describe the event, process, or person that is the subject of the lesson.

2. Students brainstorm one or more possible contemporary analogies for the event or person. For example, students might compare the Cold War to a tumultuous teenage relationship or the President of the United States to the school's principal.

Tier One/Tier Two: Whole Class, Small Group, or Individualized

3. Students then create visual representations of their analogies. Students might choose from the following options:

   a. Create a Venn diagram (see Figure 7.10) to find basic similarities and differences between concept and analogy.

b. Create a mind map to connect the new concept with an analogy.

c. Create written memory models in which they elaborate on the similarities and differences involved.

d. Find a physical object that can be used as an analogy.

To Differentiate

- Ask higher-level students to brainstorm an original analogy and its resulting connections.
- Provide a specific analogy to lower-level students and ask them to brainstorm connections between the new concept and the analogy.

Application Example

Social studies: Read a short biographical article on the current United States President (http://www.whitehouse.gov/about/presidents).

1. List five to eight characteristics of the President (examples: ambitious, won election to become president, helps develop laws).

2. Create a list of five to eight characteristics of the person being compared (principal, parent, etc.).

3. Create a Venn diagram to show similarities and differences between the two people.

Figure 7.10   Venn Diagram

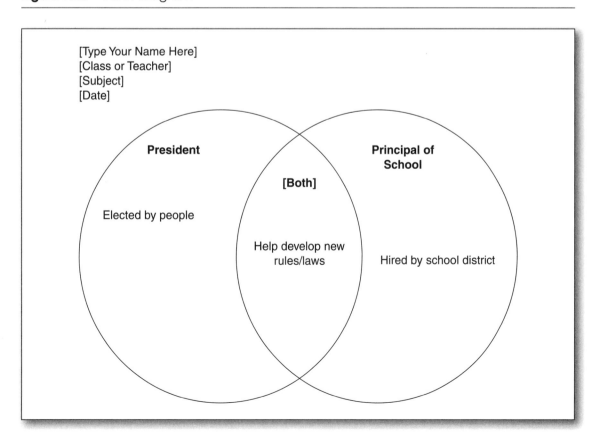

Across the Curriculum

Science teachers can use analogies to help students understand the system of the body. Figure 7.11 provides some examples.

Figure 7.11 Science Analogy

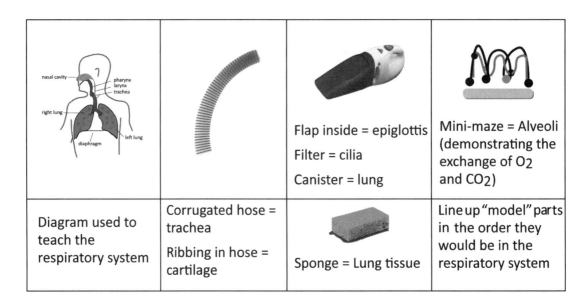

The circulatory system is like the mail delivery system:

- Arteries—Highways that the postal truck travels
- Veins—Neighborhood streets
- Blood cells—Postal trucks
- Nutrients—Mail
- Nutrients delivered to parts of the body —Mail delivered to houses
- Waste (carbon dioxide) —The envelope that gets thrown away

Assessment

English and Language Arts: Students write a paragraph to explain how a new concept is similar to an analogy they have generated.

- Include and explain at least three similarities.
- Include one to two limitations of the analogy (how the concept is unlike the analogy).

Rubric: Connect Similarities and Differences Between New Concept and Analogy

Category	1	2	3	4
Identify similarities and differences between new concept and analogy.	Does not make connections between new concept and analogy.	Distinguishes general similarities and differences between concept and analogy.	Elaborates on similarities and differences between concept and analogy.	Creates new analogies for the concept.

ADDITIONAL INTERVENTIONS FOR ■ INCREASING RECALL AND RECOGNITION

Excerpted from *Memorization and Test Taking Strategies for the Differentiated, Inclusive and RTI Classroom*, Susan Gingras Fitzell, 2010.

Many students with learning disabilities struggle with memory deficits. Primarily, they forget information they need to do well on tests or to do the higher-level thinking required for problem solving, analysis, and synthesis. For example, if students can't remember basic math facts, even if they have a calculator at their disposal, they will take longer to complete a test, thereby impacting their test scores (Levine, 2003, p. 113).

Students are using up working memory space with basic calculations rather than higher-level thinking skills. Those who struggle to remember the details of a story cannot draw inferences from those details because they can't remember the sequence of events or what happened in various parts of the story.

Remembering the details and foundation of what is being taught is critical to comprehending, applying, and analyzing that content. A Tier Two intervention strategy to differentiate instruction for students struggling to remember information in the classroom is to teach short-term memory strategies.

Chunking Information

Teach students to *chunk information* (Miller, 1956). The brain can only hold seven pieces of information at a time in short-term memory. The only way we can sometimes get away with more than seven facts is if we "chunk" related information. One way to chunk is to use color to categorize, group, and combine. For example, If we have eight or nine things, we might be able to use color to make it more like seven if some of those things go together.

For example, five facts about short-term memory might be green, five facts about working memory could be brown, and five facts about long-term memory could be black.

Paraphrase Immediately

Another strategy to enhance short-term memory so information is not gone in two seconds is to have a student paraphrase what has just been taught (Furukawa, 1978). For example, after you teach something important, ask a volunteer to paraphrase that information for the class. Most likely, your students will not repeat the information in the same words you used, so the students' rendition will be novel to the brain. This strategy only takes seconds to do, yet it lets your students hear the information again, in a different way, with a different voice. The brain likes novelty and will remember the information better.

Paraphrase One Hour Later

Ask your students to paraphrase information shared earlier in the day (Shugarman & Hurst, 1986). When they take something you taught an hour ago and bring it back into play, it returns to short-term memory and is then pushed into working memory. Using this paraphrasing strategy in your classrooms will help students to remember what you are teaching. Of course, you may need to adjust the length of the delay to fit your class schedule. The key here is returning to the information and repeating it differently.

Whisper It

Rehearsal is a strategy that we've been using in education for years (Shugarman & Hurst, 1986). One rehearsal strategy is to have students stop after you share an important fact and whisper the important information three times. The repetition and the whispering help them to remember the fact. Whispering under one's breath is a powerful tool.

Make a Rulebook

One of the best ways to help kids remember rules is to make a *rulebook* (Levine, 2003, p. 96) for your subject.

- Use two-column pages and split the rules for clarity.
- Label one column *If* and the other column *Then*.
- For example, in the *If* column, we might say "$x^2 = 4$" while the *Then* column would say "2." Or *If* "simple present verb" *Then* "modal + simple present verb".
- You can do this for most subject areas.

Applying rules is a simple strategy, as long as the rules are clear.

Draw It So That You'll Know It!

Condense information into a picture and embrace the power of color. Teachers often present information verbally and linguistically. However, many of our students are visual learners. A substantial amount of our brainpower is devoted to visual processing. When teachers add a visual component to what they are teaching, student recall increases (Levine, 2003, p. 95).

For example, after teaching for five or six minutes, or up to ten minutes in a high school class, give students three to five minutes to draw a picture, diagram, or symbol of what they just learned. This strategy takes the verbal linguistic information we just taught and turns it into visual information in the brain. The brain will process and use visual information in a different way, which, in turn, helps students better remember what has been taught.

When we use drawing exercises in the classroom, we often encounter resistance from students. They complain that they can't draw. One way to address this is to draw badly when we draw in the classroom. If we draw well, students will be intimidated and refuse to try. Use stick figure drawings and emphasize the importance of simple line drawings over drawing well. The point is to create an image that helps us remember what we've learned, not to get graded on our art.

If students say they can't draw, pair them up with someone who doesn't mind drawing. It would be a shame to lose students because of their initial resistance to doing something so different from what they are used to doing in school.

The brain has a huge capacity for visual processing, so the visual component of our memory is very powerful (Levine, 2003, p. 110).

Snapshot Devices

Another way to present information visually is to use a snapshot device. A snapshot device is a picture with all of the things you have taught in it. It's a scene, not just a collection of individual pictures. Snapshot devices take the concepts we have already talked about to another level; their purpose is to take a snapshot of information and represent it visually so students will remember it (Ehren, 2000).

For instance, you've taught about how the West was settled and explained that certain inventions were involved, such as the six-shooter, the windmill, the sod house, the locomotive, and barbed wire. If you draw pictures of a six-shooter, a windmill, and a sod house with no way to relate these things to each other, then you are drawing "unconnected" images. With a snapshot device, you take the information and make it into a scene to think about. Students will remember the cowboy with the six-shooters and the train coming down the hill behind the sod house. They will see the scene in their mind's eye (Ewy, 2003, pp. 29, 109, 165; Hyerle, 2009; Pehrsson, 1989) (see Figure 7.12).

Figure 7.12 Snapshot Device

Assessing With Visuals

When students engage in drawing what they learned, teachers have an opportunity to walk around the room and assess understanding by looking at students' drawings and asking questions for clarification. Document your observations, and you will have a form of authentic and immediate ongoing assessment.

■ IDENTIFY SIMILARITIES AND DIFFERENCES

Across the United States, seventh and eighth graders read S. E. Hinton's *The Outsiders*. The book, set in the 1950s, has relevance for today's youth. However, to youth of the new millennium, the 1950s may seem to be ancient history. I can remember reading *The Outsiders* in high school. Whereas today students are reading that book in middle school, in the 1970s it was considered a high school text. I read it in freshman English class. I loved the book then and still consider it a masterful work that provides social, emotional, and academic learning opportunities. I remember relating to the characters and discussing correlations between the issues they faced and the issues we dealt with in the seventies. For me, a sample lesson based on *The Outsiders* to illustrate methods for identifying similarities and differences was a natural pick.

Research Background

When teachers use activities that engage students in identifying similarities and differences, students achieve percentile gains of up to 46% in proficiency (Gregory, 2008).

Learning Objectives

- To distinguish the characteristics of printed materials based on comparative observation
- To create analogies between characters in a piece of literature and characters in students' everyday lives, thus incorporating more than one layer of connection to enhance long-term memory and critical thinking skills
- To engage the student in higher-ordered learning processes involving differentiation and analysis

Addresses These Nonresponder Indicators

- The student has Attention Deficit Disorder.
- The student has difficulty processing information in a way that is personally meaningful.
- The student has difficulty with higher-order thinking such as problem solving and comparing and contrasting.
- The student has trouble determining the similarities and differences in text and concrete lessons, resulting in gaps in achievement.
- The student fails to activate prior knowledge (has difficulty retrieving information previously learned).

- The student is unable to connect new information with what was previously learned.
- The student has poor auditory short-term memory.
- The student has trouble remembering what the teacher says in class.

Materials Needed

- A work of literature; for example, a short story.
- Social studies teachers might consider using key characters in a historical story.
- Science teachers might use this approach when studying concepts that have a human element. For example, one might take the activists on both sides of a land use issue, stem cell research, or green energy versus fossil fuels as a basis for comparison.

Approximate Time Frame for Completion

This lesson plan may take more than one class period, depending on class length.

- Whole group strategy (character study): 15 to 30 minutes
- Tier Two and Tier Three practice: 10 minutes or less, depending on available time
- Resulting discussion or extension learning: variable

Intervention Procedure and Scripts

Tier One/Whole Class

1. Give students any of the following:
   a. Characters from a short story
   b. Characters from a novel such as *The Outsiders*
   c. Key people discussed in a textbook who represent a time period

2. List the characters on the board.

3. Tell students to draw correlations between the characters on the list and people in their own lives. For example, you might ask, "What peer group would the characters be hanging with at our school?" (see Figure 7.13).

4. Once students have determined parallels between characters on the list and people in their lives, group the characters based on common features, personalities, politics, ideology, or other features.

5. Using Venn diagrams or mind maps, list similarities and differences between the groups in the story, text, or historical period and groups students have personal experience with today.

Figure 7.13 *The Outsiders* Characters

Randy Anderson
Johnny Cade
Darrel (Darry) Curtis
Ponyboy Curtis
Sodapop Curtis
Paul Holden
Johnnycakes
Marcia
Two-bit Matthews
Keith Matthews
Buck Merrill
Steve Randle
Sandy
Bob Sheldon
Curley Shepard
Tim Shepard
Mr. Syme
Cherry Valance
Dally Winston
Jerry Wood

The Outsiders: **What peer group would they be hanging with at our school?**

> *Note:* Students could duplicate the model on the board on their own blank copy of a Venn Diagram or on a group copy.

6. Have students create stick figure or line drawing representations of the differences between the groups.

Tier One/Tier Two/Small Group

Here is an example of how we might differentiate instruction at Tier One, as well as use best practice research-based strategies as an intervention for students who have difficulty with reading comprehension, reading recall, and analytical thinking.

1. List the characters from *The Outsiders* on the board.

2. Ask students to imagine that the characters from the book are their age and in their grade.

3. Ask students to identify where they might be hanging out at school and who they might be hanging with if they were the Greasers or the Socs. Where might a 13-year-old Mr. Syme hang out?

4. List their pairs on the board.

5. Now that students have categorized and paired the book character with someone from their peer group and social world, ask students to compare and contrast the characters and their peer groups. See Figure 7.14 for an example of how to visually represent this exercise.

   a. How are the greasers the same as _____ from our school?
   b. How are they different from students here?

Figure 7.14 Similarities and Differences Form *(The Outsiders)*

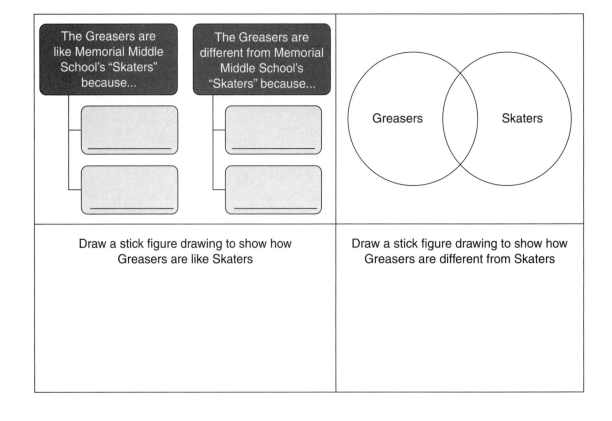

The Greasers are like Memorial Middle School's "Skaters" because...

The Greasers are different from Memorial Middle School's "Skaters" because...

Greasers   Skaters

Draw a stick figure drawing to show how Greasers are like Skaters

Draw a stick figure drawing to show how Greasers are different from Skaters

To Differentiate

1. Group students in mixed-ability triads to list similarities and differences.

2. Allow students to choose between the following activities:
   a. Illustrate the differences between characters then and now by creating meaningful symbols to represent the differences.
   b. Create analogies using the characters: *Ponyboy is to _____ as _____ is to _____; Greasers are to Socs as _____ are to _____.*

Across the Curriculum

For social studies instruction, take the topic of immigration. In the U.S. History and History Standards for Grades 5–12 (National Center for History in the Schools, 1996), Standard 2 for Era 6 is "Massive immigration after 1870 and how new social patterns, conflicts, and ideas of national unity developed amid growing cultural diversity." One of the strands in this standard is to assess the challenges, opportunities, and contributions of different immigrant groups.

Have students identify

- the new students in their school;
- new communities in their city, region, or state; and
- any relatives or friends who immigrated to the United States.

How are today's "new kids in town" the same as immigrants from the late 1800s? How might they be different? Were opportunities the same or different? (See Figure 7.15.)

Figure 7.15   Similarities and Differences Form (Centuries)

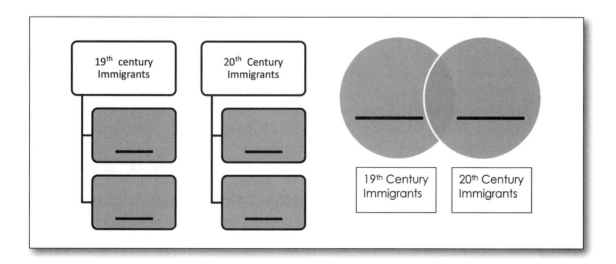

Assessment

Rubric: Connect Similarities and
Differences between Literature and Student Lives

Category	1	2	3	4
Similarities and Differences	Misses similarities or differences between characters in the text and individuals or groups in his or her personal world.	Broadly notes, but does not elaborate on, similarities or differences between characters in the text and individuals or groups in his or her personal world.	Elaborates on similarities or differences between characters in the text and individuals or groups in his or her personal world.	Expands upon the analogies to draw parallels between the two worlds and deepen understanding of the characters in the literature piece.
Likenesses and Differences from Specific People or Groups in Students' Lives	Does not specify or detail clear similarities and differences between characters in the text to people in his or her personal world.	Specifies and details clear similarities and differences between characters in the text and people in his or her personal world, but does not elaborate on those differences.	Elaborates on similarities and differences between characters in the text and people in his or her personal world.	Expands upon the analogies to explain how the details in the literature piece are similar to the details of the lives of people in the student's personal world and why that correlation is significant to understanding the reading.

■ TEACHING SUMMARIZING SKILLS: DELETE-SUBSTITUTE-KEEP

Summarizing is a skill that not only has a substantial effect on student learning but is of lifelong utility. It is also a skill that students have significant struggles with. One of the worst consequences of a lack of summarizing skill is the ease with which students will mistakenly plagiarize. Early in my teaching career, I noticed that when students were assigned a summarizing assignment, they would simply copy sentences from the book, rearranged. Rather than read a sentence and tell it in their own words, they simply switched the wording around.

Not only were they simply copying, they were doing it poorly. When I'd question their methodology and suggest that they were plagiarizing, they were adamant that they were not plagiarizing because what they wrote did not look exactly the same as the text from which they were copying. Finally, through trial and error, I discovered that if students read a paragraph, then covered it, then stated what they read in one sentence, they could often summarize the paragraph in their own words. This sample lesson plan takes this basic concept and varies it to provide a few different options for teaching students how to summarize.

Research Background

Summarizing allows students to reframe their understanding by identifying key facts and concepts and filing information away in long-term memory in a more concise form. Much research has been done on the efficacy of summarizing. Marzano, Pickering, and Pollack do an excellent job of compiling and presenting that research in teacher-friendly terms (Marzano et al., 2001).

Learning Objectives

- To identify the main ideas in various types of writing
- To create topic sentences to present an overall summary of a piece of writing
- To apply a specific summarization strategy (Delete-Substitute-Keep) to various types of writing
- To synthesize information and present it in a way that is meaningful to them
- To enhance their comprehension through summarization
- To apply summarization strategies in many curricular areas
- To recognize the importance of summarization in real-world applications

Addresses These Nonresponder Indicators

- The student has difficulty summarizing information without plagiarizing.
- The student has difficulty filtering out important facts and concepts and organizing information into an abstract form.
- The student has difficulty processing information gained from reading in a way that is personally meaningful.
- The student has notetaking deficiencies.
- The student has poor reading recall.
- The student has processing disorders.
- The student struggles to effectively use words to express organized and complete thoughts in writing.

Materials Needed

- Literature (magazine or newspaper articles, textbooks, poetry, novels, short stories, nonfiction and fiction texts, websites, blogs)
- A soft ball or Koosh ball

Approximate Time Frame for Completion

- Story retell: 5 to 10 minutes
- Direct instruction: 15 to 20 minutes (variable, depending on article length and student participation)
- Jigsaw: 20 minutes (variable, depending on article length and student understanding)
- Independent practice: 20 to 30 minutes (variable, depending on article length and student understanding)

Intervention Procedure and Scripts

Tier One: Whole Class

Story Retell

A quick, easy way to introduce summarization is to do a story retell. This strategy helps students identify main ideas. You can use it with a story that the class recently read, a movie, or something as basic as a fairy tale. You could even use it to review a class lesson. The key is to choose something that all students are familiar with so that everyone can participate in a whole class environment.

1. Have the students stand in a circle. Give one student a soft ball (Koosh or Nerf).

2. The student holding the ball begins to retell the story with one beginning sentence. He then throws the ball to another student.

3. The next student tells another important event in the story and throws the ball to another student.

4. The students continue to pass the ball and tell a story event until they get to the end of the story.

Delete-Substitute-Keep Strategy (Marzano et al., 2001, pp. 19–26)

1. Place a sample article on an overhead projector or computer display so that all students can see clearly. The typeface should be 24 points or larger.

2. Read the article aloud, and then have students reread the article silently.

3. Turn off the projector. Ask students to provide one sentence to summarize the article. List all suggestions on the board.

4. Turn the projector back on. Have students give suggestions for unnecessary words or sentences to delete. Do the same thing for redundant sentences. Cross deletions out in red.

5. Go through the article and substitute superordinate terms; for example, *trees* for *pines*, *oaks*, and *maples*. Do this in blue.

6. Reread the article without all of the deleted items. Refer back to the one-sentence summaries and choose the topic sentence that fits best.

7. Write the summary, beginning with the topic sentence.
   a. Cover the article and have students provide key ideas in their own words.
   b. When they get stuck or think they are finished, they may refer back to the article to ensure they have included all of the necessary information and to check for accuracy.

Tier Two: Small Group

The Delete-Substitute-Keep strategy is an excellent partner activity as well as a student/specialist intervention activity.

Tier One: Small Group

Jigsaw

The Jigsaw strategy (Marzano et al., 2001, p. 30) is a great way to help students practice summarization skills. Each student (or group) is assigned a section of an article, chapter, or book (the whole puzzle). He or she is responsible for reading that section (the piece) and teaching the rest of the class about that part. By teaching it to others, students will have to convey clearly the main ideas of their reading to ensure that all students understand all pieces of the puzzle.

1. Place students in mixed-ability groups.

2. Assign each group a section of the reading.

3. Students thoroughly read their assigned piece.

4. Students apply the summarization strategies (see above) modeled by the teacher.

5. Students report their summaries to the rest of the class.

If students do this correctly, they will have a complete understanding of the entire reading, even though they did not read the entire piece themselves. They will love not having to read the entire passage and thus will be motivated to do a good job!

Tier Two/Tier Three: Independent Practice

Blind Summarizing

In my work teaching summarizing skills to students with learning challenges, I struggled to find a way to help them summarize without repeating what they read verbatim. Finally, one day when at my wit's end, I told a student to read a paragraph.

After he read the paragraph, I made him flip the book over. Once he could not see the text, I asked, "Now, tell me what you read in one sentence." It worked. Some students would initially go blank. However, with persistence, modeling, and practice, students started to be successful with reading one paragraph and then summarizing it in one sentence without that paragraph in sight.

I taught my students that if they could summarize each paragraph they read in one sentence orally and then write it down on paper, they would have a summary of a page or an article when they were done without the danger of plagiarizing. With continual practice, by the end of a semester, all my students could write a summary of an article without plagiarizing. Following is a variation of the process.

1. Skim the article once.

2. Then reread one paragraph at a time.

3. After each paragraph, cover up the paragraph and summarize it in one sentence. Then do one of the following:

   a. Say the sentence to a scribe.
   b. Say the sentence into a digital recorder.
   c. Write the sentence down without worrying about spelling or grammar. Correct that later. It's more important to get the words down on paper before they are forgotten.

5. When finished summarizing each paragraph with one sentence, combine those sentences into a written summary.

6. Add a topic sentence and a conclusion.

7. Refer back to the article for additional ideas and to check for accuracy. Be careful to avoid the temptation to directly copy sentences from the article into the summary.

> *Note:* There are times when one sentence per paragraph may be inefficient or ineffective. Start students with short articles or sections of text that are manageable. When students progress to more difficult texts, they may choose to summarize more than one paragraph at a time.

Optional Supports

- Create a small Summarizing Cue Card (see Figure 7.16 on page 161) that students can keep on their desk or in their folder to remind them of these steps:

  1. Delete unnecessary words or sentences.

  2. Substitute superordinate terms (for example, *trees* for *pines, oaks,* and *maples*).

  3. Select or create a topic sentence.

- You may want to provide students with a checklist for their summary writing (see Figure 7.17 on page 162):

  1. Does your topic sentence synthesize all the important information?

  2. Are the main ideas clear and accurate?

  3. Is your summary concise?

  4. Does your summary maintain the author's voice?

  5. Did you replace superordinate terms?

To Differentiate

- Provide students with highlighting tape to highlight information to be summarized in textbooks and magazines.
- Have students lay an overhead transparency over the text and highlight text on the transparency. Students may need a clipboard or paper clip to make sure the transparency doesn't move.
- To provide choice, students can use preselected articles or choose their own. If they are choosing their own articles, help them pick materials at an appropriate reading level in order to provide an appropriate challenge while avoiding frustration.

Across the Curriculum

This strategy can be applied to all curriculum areas. Here are some examples:

- In social studies, use it to preview an entire chapter. Each group can "become the expert" on a particular section of the chapter (or even the entire book, depending on your purpose).
- In science, each group can present a different research study about a particular concept.
- In math, students can read about different strategies to solving the same type of problem.
- In physical education, students can read and present about different techniques to achieve optimal health.

As long as there is something to read, students can practice these summarizing strategies!

For Independent Writing Assignments

The Delete-Substitute-Keep strategy most directly lends itself to individual writing assignments in which students are using literary resources to obtain information. However, the Retelling strategy also works well; just have the student write down their retelling! Students can also write down their individual portion of a jigsaw.

For Independent Reading Assignments (Literature or Content Area)

All three strategies (Retelling, Jigsaw, and Delete-Substitute-Keep) can be applied to independent reading assignments.

For Group Brainstorming and Mind Map Creation

All three summarizing strategies can be applied to group brainstorming and mind mapping. Students can help one another to understand the process and further develop their mind mapping or sequencing skills.

Extension

Students may select their own articles to find material that meets their interest and academic ability level. They may even seek out interesting pieces that they would like the class to jigsaw.

Assessment

Rubric: Summarizing Pieces of Literature

Category	1	2	3	4
Topic Sentence	Writes a topic sentence that focuses on details and does not summarize.	Generally states the main ideas in the literature but does not narrow it to one overall topic sentence.	Identifies the main idea but does not synthesize all of the necessary information.	Succinctly hones in on the main idea with a topic sentence that synthesizes all of the relevant information, creating an umbrella for the rest of the paragraph.
Main Ideas	Does not discern main ideas from the details.	Picks out main ideas but includes some details.	Identifies the main ideas.	Identifies and synthesizes the main ideas.
Deleting and Substituting	Does not differentiate between necessary and unnecessary information and lacks substitute words; struggles to find words to substitute.	Deletes and substitutes some of the unnecessary and redundant information, but struggles to substitute with terms that are more general.	Deletes and substitutes unnecessary and redundant information.	Creatively deletes and substitutes all unnecessary and redundant information from the literature while maintaining the integrity of the author's writing.

Figure 7.16 Summarizing Cue Card

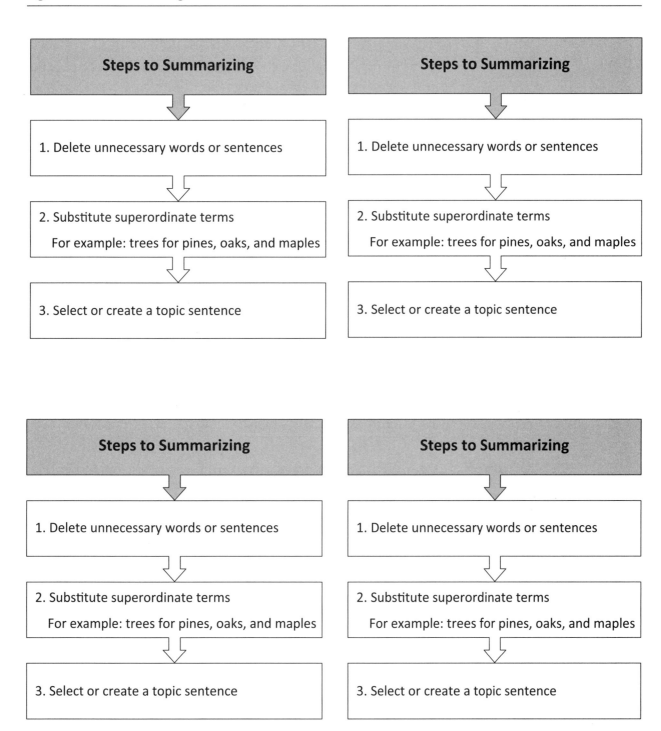

Figure 7.17 Quick Steps to Check Your Summary Cue Card

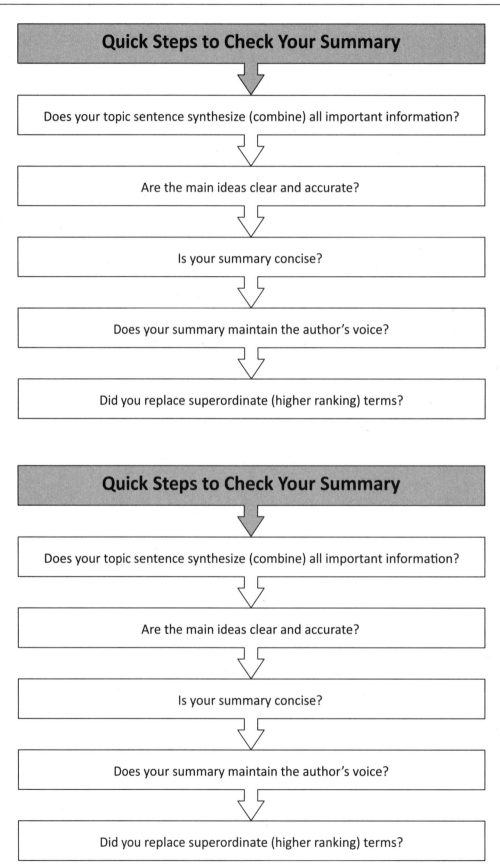

8

Fitzell Acceleration Centers as an RTI Strategy

As described in previous chapters of this text, there are varieties of approaches for providing RTI interventions in the general classroom. This section explores acceleration centers (Nilson, 1998) as a vehicle to delivering Tier Two, and possibly Tier Three, interventions. This approach is one of the most effective formats for addressing a wide range of abilities in the general education classroom. The Fitzell Acceleration Center is not a product that can be purchased; rather, it is a concept and process for center teaching at the secondary level. Its basic features are presented in Figure 8.1.

The benefit of the acceleration center model is that it is a powerful strategy for

- differentiation;
- responding to student learning (or nonlearning);
- teaching in the inclusive classroom;
- addressing multiple ability levels in the classroom; and
- correcting student apathy and lack of motivation.

Acceleration center teaching is an advanced teaching structure. It can be combined with any other pedagogy or teaching method.

Figure 8.1

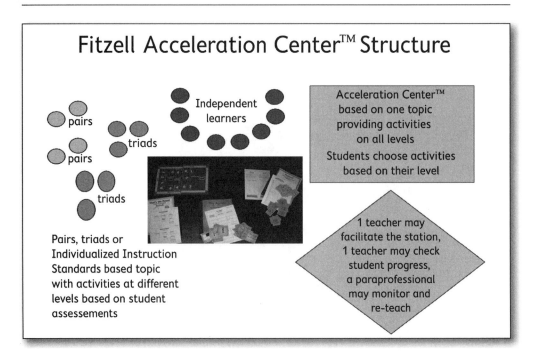

In broad terms, acceleration centers incorporate a "station" in a corner of the room, a piece of the room, a setup in the room, or a crate in the room. Its purpose is to have students focus on one topic. That topic might address the standards on which your students did not do well on the state test last year. On the other hand, it might be an aspect of your curriculum that you need to repeat for some students who struggle, while at the same time providing advanced material for those students that need to be challenged beyond the standard curriculum. The goal is to give all your students an opportunity to succeed. It's also a perfect structure for delivering Tier Two interventions as well as supporting Tier One (general classroom) and, where possible, Tier Three interventions.

I remember spending an entire week creating a learning center on plants many years ago. Every night I was cutting out leaves, flowers, and petals. I made hands-on activities using clothespins and construction paper. I spent hours upon hours on this learning center. Friday was the big day. I introduced the center to the students and explained the instructions. I had that sense of excitement and fulfillment a teacher experiences after having worked extremely hard to create what he or she feels should be an award-winning lesson plan. My students finished the center in 45 minutes. All those hours of preparation and it was over in 45 minutes!

Who has the time for that today? My observation is that, generally speaking, teachers do not use learning centers anymore. We just don't have the time to prepare learning centers using this paradigm. Additionally, secondary teachers rarely use centers. They may be used in some science classes, but for the most part, it's a foreign concept and considered "elementary."

ACCELERATION CENTERS: ■
A BETTER ALTERNATIVE

An acceleration center is not the same as an elementary learning center. It's a combination of several "station" methods. If you have ever created a learning center, implemented an Accelerated Reader program, or if you are familiar with SRA (Science Research Associates) Individualized Direct Instruction for Reading Mastery, you have worked with different types of centers. The acceleration center takes the best of each of these models and combines them into a model that is appropriate at the secondary level.

The concept of an acceleration center is similar to that of a learning center except that teachers do not create a separate center for every unit they are teaching. They don't have a holiday center, for example, or a math center created for a specific lesson plan. Instead, teachers focus on a curriculum strand, taken from their state standard, that aligns with the Tier Two intervention needs of students in the general classroom. The activities in the center range from the very basic skills in the strand (Tier Two interventions for struggling students) to the highest level skills (Tier One activities and strategies for all students) and possibly even college-level material (enrichment curricula) if students can reach that far. For students who need Tier Two interventions, the focus of the center could be based on one of their areas of difficulty: finding similarities and differences, understanding cause and effect, foundational concepts required for algebra, or the like. The focus of the center is determined by assessment data collected by the general education teacher (and the RTI team, where applicable).

Once developed, each center remains for the entire year, and beyond.

- You make it once and use it all year.
- You prepare it once and possibly add to it during the year.
- The only maintenance required is student assessment and reassignment.

Teachers put a tremendous amount of thought into how they will individualize instruction to meet their students' needs, meet curriculum benchmarks, and state standards, as well as provide Tier Two interventions. The challenge, and a benefit, to implementing acceleration centers is that it requires significant advanced preparation—once. After you gather the materials and create a center, the preparation is done and minimal planning and maintenance are required.

With an acceleration center, teachers

- use standards-based topics and activities aimed at reaching all learning levels while at the same time providing Tier Two interventions;
- use authentic assessments and progress monitoring to determine student learning levels;
- assess students to identify how they are doing on a daily or weekly basis; and
- use the data to determine assignments needed in the acceleration center at all learning levels in the classroom.

You might have students working in pairs or triads, or you might have independent learners. In a co-teaching environment, one teacher may facilitate a center activity while the other teacher coaches a small group or an individual student, teaches half the class a minilesson, administers one-minute assessments, or performs any number of relevant tasks. The beauty of using a co-teaching model for implementation of acceleration centers is that while one teacher is facilitating the station, the other adult in the room could be teaching an intervention lesson.

An acceleration center is a designated area, file crate, file drawer, or pocketed bulletin board that provides students with standards-based learning activities at a range of ability levels so that students can focus on achieving standards. Ideally, acceleration centers use as few handouts as possible. They are activities, at varying learning levels, which consider and address student learning styles, needs, and necessary interventions.

Activities may be hands-on, involve manipulatives, include creativity, or come in the form of investigations or challenges that require critical thinking skills. Acceleration centers may incorporate computer-based instruction, utilizing the few computers in the classroom in a way that is impractical with the whole-class teaching model. The acceleration center may be focused on a particular skill area or on weak areas identified through previous test results.

For example, secondary students are consistently weak in the areas of fractions and measurements. An acceleration center focused on fractions and decimals might include activities as basic as matching numeric fractions to a fraction pie (supporting Tier Two interventions) or as advanced as the use of decimals in calculus (Tier One and at or above grade level). This fraction- and decimal-based center would provide students who are not making adequate yearly progress a forum for accelerating those skills (Tier Two interventions), while also providing students who are at the highest level of achievement the opportunity to reach their potential.

Teachers choose pockets of time during the week to assign students to work with an acceleration center. If using centers for Tier Two interventions, a minimum of 30 minutes twice per week should be dedicated to center work. Students visit the center to complete activities assigned to them based on current assessment data derived from progress monitoring (for example, exit cards or current curriculum-based measurement).

Acceleration centers are governed by pre-taught and practiced rules and procedures that require students to be responsible and accountable for their own growth. Students benefit from individual and small group work just as they do with SRA, Accelerated Reader, or with any number of computer programs that promote skill building and acceleration. These programs provide a forum for presenting information to students in a way that is not always possible with a whole class lesson, allowing teachers to spend time with students individually or in small groups. It also opens up an opportunity for action research, observations of student learning and behavior, or ongoing immediate assessment.

The acceleration center model allows you to take a certain time period within the course of a week to focus at the basic level for those students who aren't responding. Those who need intensified instruction in foundational skills are now able to get what they need. Later, they are able to participate during a whole class lesson.

What happens to those students who already understand? While some students are working on the basics, these students can work at a higher grade level on the same topic. Station teaching using acceleration centers allows you to reach many different learning levels in your classroom at the same time, effectively and efficiently.

ADDRESSING THE CHALLENGES OF IMPLEMENTING FITZELL ACCELERATION CENTERS ■

Prep time: The biggest challenge teachers face when implementing acceleration centers is that they require significant one-time preparation. Ideally, teachers can find time during a professional development or summer workshop day, or choose to spend a few days after school to prepare a center. Once the preparation is complete, you don't have to do it again, and you will have a center that can be used over and over again. You might add to it or adjust it, but you won't have to create a new lesson from scratch.

Keeping students occupied: For acceleration centers to work effectively, teachers need to have options for students who finish early. If we try to make sure that students are finishing their assignment at the same time, we will become frustrated with the process. It is simply not possible for all students to finish their center activities at the same time. When students have finished their goal charts and they've done the things they're supposed to accomplish, have options available for them to choose from.

Wide range of abilities: You might have one or more groups of students working independently from the teacher, so if four or five different levels of students are working on different levels of assignments and there is only one adult in the room, you will have students working on their own. If you have a co-teacher or specialist enhancing the instructional services for the students, providing either special education services or RTI interventions, the other adults' skills are maximized with the center approach. I realize that the option for collaborative teaching may or may not be viable in your classroom or school. Essentially, success depends on student behavior, initiative, ability to focus, and student understanding of teacher expectations and related consequences.

Behavior management: Teachers must have a good handle on discipline and strict rules about how time is managed and how students should behave during center time. Students need to be taught how to behave when working with acceleration centers; otherwise, they might think it's a free-for-all, especially if they have never worked with centers before. We really need to be clear about our expectations and enforce them.

Some teachers struggle with implementing center teaching because of the classroom management challenge the model poses. In reality, when students understand teacher expectations, are given time to practice the rules of engagement, and those rules are enforced while providing incentive for success, teachers actually have fewer discipline problems. Students behave better when they are engaged.

Noise level: During center teaching, you may experience a higher level of noise in the classroom than usual. Decide which students should be partners;

ascertain which students will mix best, and put them together deliberately. You may say, "You can work with so-and-so" or "I don't want you working with so-and-so." Possibly separate the talkative students and keep them apart. The trade-off for a quiet classroom is having students who are engaged in the learning process rather than experiencing frustration in their learning.

Acceleration Centers Respond to All Learners

The acceleration center approach allows students to work at their own ability levels. When teaching in diverse classrooms with a wide range of ability levels, few things work better to bridge the gap than station teaching. With acceleration centers, students can work at their ability level on either individualized or small group activities focused on accelerating their progress in meeting curriculum goals and state standards.

When implementing acceleration centers, start small. Start with one standard and one center with multiple activities at varying levels. I've worked with teachers who get very excited about these ideas and immediately start planning three different centers, or a center per teaching unit. I would not advise starting out with more than one center. Start with one. You will be less likely to become overwhelmed with the planning and prep work involved, students will have time to practice using centers, and the bugs can be worked out before a new acceleration center is planned.

■ ACCELERATION CENTER FLOWCHART

At a recent workshop that focused on understanding and creating acceleration centers, a group of teachers produced a flowchart that presents the implementation process in steps. Credit is due to Ms. Jones, Ms. Johnston, Ms. Tribula, and Ms. Whim from Woodington Middle School in Kinston, North Carolina, for the initial version of this flowchart (see Figure 8.2).

■ ACCELERATION CENTER INSTRUCTIONS

Step 1: Decide on Area of Need

The first step to creating an acceleration center is to determine your students' area or areas of need and decide where to focus your attention. Let's take a look at some subject-specific areas of need that you may consider addressing.

If you are teaching science, look at your state test scores and determine which questions resulted in the most common student errors. According to the National Assessment of Educational Progress (Grigg, Lauko, & Brockway, 2006), 43% of American fourth to eighth graders in urban school districts do not have a basic understanding of science. This is a national challenge. Test results may indicate that students cannot read basic charts. We might also have students who cannot follow the instructions of simple experiments. If so, we could create a center focused on Grade Level Expectations (GLEs) in the science standard that require students to be able to read charts and graphs.

Figure 8.2   Acceleration Center™ Concept Map

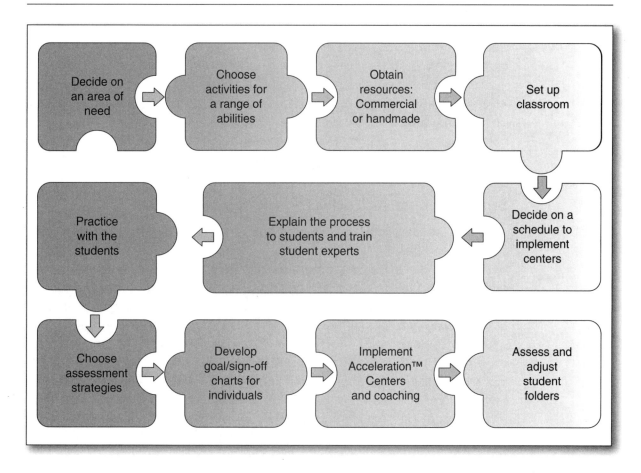

We will then add a range of assignments aimed at application of charts and graphs that at the same time provide practice in following instructions for simple experiments.

In English, students may be struggling with drawing inferences, having trouble with cause and effect, or encountering difficulty with figurative language. Examine the standards and look at the strand that includes those concepts. Consider objectives from very basic strands that students might begin to learn in earlier grades to skills required three to four years above grade level. Include a wide range of information that addresses the needs of advanced students so there is something for everyone in the acceleration center.

In math, many students have trouble with measurement, fractions, and decimals on their state tests. Using the acceleration center to provide reinforcement of concepts that are foundational to understanding math is an attractive option. For instance, scheduling center time for this purpose allows opportunities for students to use manipulatives in order to understand fractions. When you are expected to continue moving forward in math, sending students who need reinforcement time to an acceleration center for that additional study of basic concepts offers a way for those students to succeed.

For example, I have an acceleration center on fractions and decimals. It includes activities at an appropriate level for those students who can't correctly identify fractions. I may have other students who understand fractions and decimals and therefore need to be challenged to rise to the next level. For those students, I include an activity that requires using fractions and decimals to calculate the inertia required to get a roller coaster to continue along its path.

Acceleration centers include everything from the very basic to the highest level of skill. These activities are *all* in the center, *all* at the same time, and *all* on the same topic. We don't change topics every month. The center's primary purpose is to focus on one strand in a standard that is critical to student success and to lay a strong foundation for accelerating growth for all learners.

Step 2: Choose Activities for a Range of Abilities

Once we determine our area of need, the next thing to do is develop a range of activities.

For example, in English, some students could be drawing inferences, some could be working on basic cause and effect, and some students might be learning the basics of persuasive writing. Students can be separated into pairs or triads, with activities at their level taken from the acceleration center.

Other students may already be good at drawing inferences, and they may score high on tests in that area. Suppose they are proficient at persuasive writing. Maybe they can write a nonfiction book or a short story for publication. Perhaps they can create and maintain a blog. Websites such as http://www.edublogs.org offer space for teachers to encourage students to start and maintain a blog as a writing motivator. This type of activity is great for all students, but for the more advanced students, the potential for challenge is an excellent motivator.

Some of your math students might not understand the basics of measurement. This will hinder them during full-class lessons when you're trying to get them to build on those skills. Student needs are not being met, and the students begin to fall behind. As the math teacher, you might design a center that requires students to measure tables, chairs, and other objects in the room with a ruler or tape measure.

I've heard university professors say that a significant number of students with high SAT and ACT math scores, including some who have taken advanced placement calculus, cannot apply much of what they should know to their engineering courses. This is because they memorized the formulas without really understanding what the math means. We can use the same kind of fun tools for these higher-level students: manipulatives, algebra tiles, even Tinker Toys (based on the Pythagorean progressive right triangle) that we use for the students at other levels to help them to develop math models, solve problems, and understand the math (Strange, 1996). Create an acceleration center that supports math application and short answer items.

One of your acceleration center activities could be to have copies of previous state test questions for students to review. They can highlight the words they don't know, come up with a creative way to learn those words, and teach those words to another person. While some students are working on vocabulary words from the past test, the students who understand the vocabulary and are ready to move on start working on their SAT or ACT vocabulary.

A group of teachers had been teaching their students vocabulary words frequently used in testing: words such as *evaluate*, *compare*, *contrast*, *discuss*, and *enumerate*. However, when the state test results came back, they found that their students' scores were about the same as the previous year. They downloaded the previous year's state test and asked the students to highlight all the words in the test that they didn't know. When they reviewed the student-generated lists, they realized that many words on the state test were unfamiliar to the students. To solve this problem, they incorporated these troublesome words into their curriculum. They also focused on increasing test vocabulary using a variety of strategies, including peer teaching and role-play skits.

Suppose you want to work on critical thinking skills in multiplication. As a center activity, you might have students listen to "Multiplication Rock." One of the best ways for students to learn their multiplication tables is to sing them. This could be a powerful center activity.

Students with well-developed critical thinking skills could practice advanced writing by composing a letter to a government official or the author of a favorite novel. This activity could be differentiated for students at varying levels of ability. Experience has shown that when students write to someone they look up to, or about an issue concerning which they feel strongly, they put more effort into the project. When they receive a reply, even if it's a form letter, they are on top of the world.

Step 3: Obtain Resources, Commercial or Handmade

I don't advocate that teachers stay up all night coming up with ideas, lesson plans, and materials for centers. We don't have to reinvent the wheel or create everything from scratch. There are free materials on the market and in your storage closet that are perfect for acceleration center activities. Of course, you can also purchase materials if you choose.

For example, Walch Education offers a product series for middle schools called *Building Math*. This three-book series uses hands-on investigations and group activities to excite and engage students in learning algebra and data analysis. The books *Everest Trek, Stranded!* and *Amazon Mission* (for Grades 6 through 8) guide students through simulations of climbing the world's tallest mountain, being marooned on a desert island, and navigating a mighty river basin. Students face one math challenge after another, continually building skills.

Another ready-made product that slips beautifully into acceleration centers is the Math Learning Center's *Math and the Mind's Eye* series (http://www.mathlearningcenter.org; see Figure 8.3). For example, in *Unit IX: Picturing Algebra*, students explore formulae, algebraic notation, equivalent expressions, and equations using toothpicks and algebra manipulatives. The centers are done for you; it is a hands-on way to teach an understanding of algebra and pre-algebra.

Evan-Moor Educational Publishers (http://www.evan-moor.com/centers) offers hands-on materials through Grade 7 for many of the strands we teach.

Figure 8.3 AC Example

Their center activities are called "Take it to Your Seat" centers. The center looks like a workbook; you open it up, tear out the pages, cut out and laminate the pieces, and you have a center! Though they're not free, they are inexpensive. This product is one I've used in my own acceleration centers.

In addition, www.HandsonEnglish.com has activities that make English hands-on. Although it is a website for ESL students, there are some excellent strategies for English center activities. There is a nominal subscription fee for this service.

One of the best ways to get free solutions and free activities is to do a Google search for the topic and lesson plans. For example, if you want to find hands-on lesson plans about drawing inferences, your Google search would be, *"drawing inferences" "lesson plans" "hands-on."* Take special note of search results that say *Elementary*, as these items often contain center ideas that can be adapted to the secondary classroom. This may take some time, but it's free. Another great way to find free materials is to Google websites geared to homeschoolers. Homeschooling websites have many lesson plans and activities, often free of charge. These sites also have an abundance of hands-on lesson plans.

Step 4: Arrange Your Classroom Environment for Success

Once you have identified your students' needs, settled on a center topic, and chosen a variety of appropriate activities, it's time to set up the classroom!

Note: All the remaining steps apply to both acceleration centers and flexible grouping. Flexible groups classroom Option 2 (see Figure 8.5 on page 174) and Option 3 (see Figure 8.6 on page 175) also work well for mirror and flip-flop teaching. When flip-flop teaching, the class is divided in half. Each teacher takes half the class to teach a different skill. When that lesson is over, students then switch teachers; thus they flip-flop. With mirror teaching, both teachers teach the same skill. The benefit to mirror teaching is working with two smaller groups.

One day, while coaching at a middle school in North Carolina, I entered a small classroom and found that the teachers had divided the class in half and were doing flip-flop teaching. They had arranged the desks in conference table style. The two teachers were at either end so as not to drown each other out. Because it was like a conference table with the students and teachers all very close together, they had complete behavioral control. It was one of the most effective uses of small space I've ever seen.

Develop a Class Plan for Differentiating Within Groups

Decide on a physical classroom desk and table arrangement (see Figures 8.4, 8.5, and 8.6).

- Will one room arrangement work, or will you need to have options for multiple arrangements depending on the group activity required?
- How will the class be rearranged when necessary? What will be required to accomplish rearranging the classroom?
- What routines and skills are necessary for students to learn to have the class run smoothly when we deviate from the traditional row arrangement? Have students practice moving from one room arrangement to another.
- Use a signal, either a hand gesture or a sound, to notify students of time remaining until a transition, then use the signal again when the transition needs to occur. Before any transition, remind students of behavioral expectations.

The goal in designing the classroom to be conducive to small group work is to design a structure that allows the teacher or teachers to interact quickly and easily with all students.

Things to think about:

- Will this arrangement work for all activities, or will it need to be rearranged for certain things?
- If rearrangement will be needed, how will that be accomplished? Can the students do it quickly and safely?
- Will teachers be able to see each other clearly in order to coordinate activities and communicate?

Figure 8.4

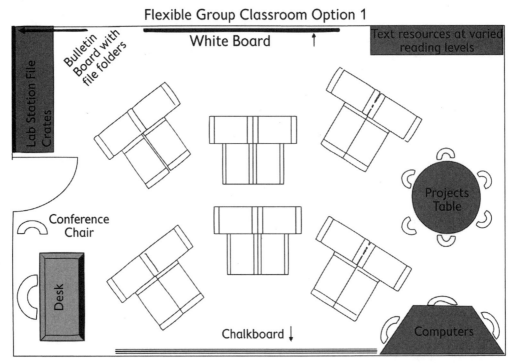

Flexible Group Classroom Option 1

24 Students - Groups of 4 + small group option for projects & computer work

Source: Fitzell Acceleration Centers™

Figure 8.5

Flexible Group Classroom Option 2

32 Students - Pairs & Divided Class with small group options

Source: Fitzell Acceleration Centers™

Figure 8.6

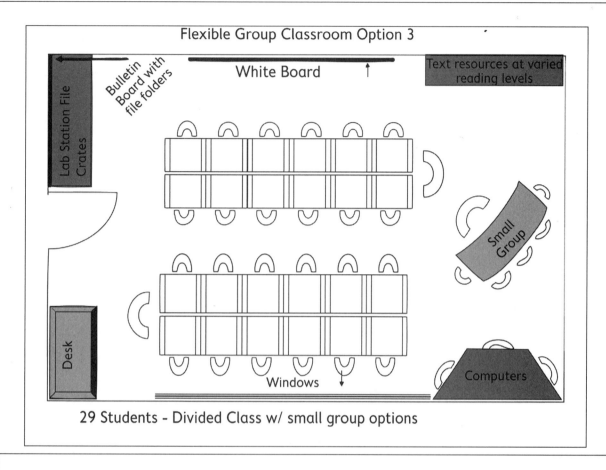

Flexible Group Classroom Option 3

Lab Station File Crates

Bulletin Board with file folders

White Board

Text resources at varied reading levels

Small Group

Desk

Windows

Computers

29 Students - Divided Class w/ small group options

Classroom Planning Handout

Use this space to sketch out your classroom arrangement ideas.

Source: Fitzell Acceleration Centers™

Step 5: Decide on a Schedule to Implement Centers

Teachers have so much material to cover that it is unlikely you can use acceleration centers every day. Most teachers don't. Some will cover curriculum material during the first four days of the week and do acceleration centers on Friday. Others may do acceleration centers two periods a week. Some teachers can divide the period in half and alternate groups. Implement centers according to your schedule. Start small and grow with your success.

Step 6: Train Student Experts

Suppose I have 10 minutes to focus on providing students with an intervention through small group or one-on-one coaching. I want that time to be uninterrupted. The last thing in the world I want during a coaching session is for students to bombard me asking, "What do I do next, Mrs. Fitzell?"; "Now what do I do, Mrs. Fitzell?"; or "Mrs. Fitzell, will you check this for me?"

A significant benefit to acceleration center teaching is having the time to work closely with students one on one or in small groups. Keeping that benefit in the face of interruptions requires that we spend time at the beginning of the process teaching students how to use centers and training student experts who can help you manage your centers.

These students are not experts on the content. They are experts on how the center works, how to check activities in and out (including inventorying materials), and what to do after completing an activity. Train the student expert to answer questions like, "I don't understand what the teacher wants me to do," "Who is my partner supposed to be?"; "What do I do next?"; and "What do I do if I'm finished?" so that students in centers do not need to interrupt the teacher.

You might even consider training your biggest, baddest, most difficult student to be your expert because that student is going to think, "Oh, I'm an expert!" I have seen some of the most difficult-to-manage students with ADHD become the most amazing peer leaders when given the opportunity. You will be astounded at how well this approach can work.

Step 7: Practice With the Students

Practice behavioral expectations for the center model. Students know how to do a handout, they know how to pretend they are following along, but they don't necessarily know how to get out of their seat, go sit with a partner, start to work, and stay on task without disrupting other students along the way. We have to teach them these skills.

I've been asked, "How can I make centers work in a 45-minute class period? There isn't enough time." My first answer is always to use timers. As teachers today, we need to be very efficient with our use of time. Teach students how to move from one activity or center to another, quickly and quietly within the classroom. Train them. Make it a contest or a game and reward them for transitioning between activities very quickly.

I have seen middle school classrooms with gifted students, students with ADHD or Asperger's syndrome, and even students with Tourette's syndrome successfully manage these movement challenges. The teachers in these classrooms have drilled the students to practice how to move the desks and regroup. The students are successful. They do it silently, they move quickly, and they finish within 15 to 20 seconds.

The teachers make it a contest. They train their students to meet the expectations and periodically give incentives like "Gosh, you guys did so well today when moving into groups that I'm going to give you . . ." some incentive. The students love it.

In high school, teachers will say, "All right, the whole class transitioned into groups in 10 seconds. None of my other classes have done it that fast." Then, in the next class, the teacher says, "Hey, my last class did it in 10 seconds. Do you think you can beat them?" Students love to meet that challenge and earn bragging rights for their class. These techniques are straight out of Dale Carnegie, but nonetheless, they work.

Step 8: Choose Assessment Strategies

When thinking about how to assess students in centers, consider assessment strategies you are already familiar with, such as accelerated reader, SRA, one-minute assessments, or the kind of short tests you might adapt from a workbook. To ensure the fidelity of an assessment, give a pretest and a posttest before students move to the next level.

On-the-spot assessment techniques that check for understanding

- Use whiteboard responses to assess.
- Exit cards (also known as "tickets to leave"). See Chapter 2 of this book for examples and explanation of exit cards.

Use whiteboards to encourage participation and for assessment

1. Every student has a whiteboard. Use a dry erase marker or wipeoff crayon. An old child-sized sock serves as eraser and for storage of markers.

2. The teacher asks a question and students write their answers on the whiteboards.

3. After a fair amount of time, the teacher asks students to hold up their boards.

4. The teacher can see how *all* students are doing with one look around the room.

This strategy eliminates blurters and allows those who need processing time to finally get it.

Exit cards

To review the application of exit cards, see the section of Chapter 2 on assessment strategies (pages 12–16). Using the results of this assessment, you can create groups based on criteria that would best support the goals of the small group activity or acceleration center.

Step 9: Use Goal Charts to Manage Accelerated Learning

This is a critical step in the implementation of acceleration centers. Use goal charts (illustrated in the Components section of this chapter, below) for each assignment to manage student learning, to individualize, and to accelerate learning.

Again, this is *critical*! Every student must have a goal chart. This aspect of acceleration centers takes preplanning. You may want to review the goal charts weekly or once every two weeks. The timing of your reviews depends on two things: how much time you spend working with the acceleration centers, and how quickly students finish their goal sheets.

Step 10: Implement Acceleration Centers and Coaching

Try an application of your chosen model. Start with small steps towards implementation. If it's overwhelming, you are probably trying to do too much all at once.

Brett and Kate, a teaching pair from Penacook, New Hampshire, decided to do just that: try it. They chose one standard strand: mastering multiples, multiplication, and division. Then they set up one center with four stations around the room to practice the strand at different levels. Each center presented a challenge activity using a different game format.

In a debriefing session afterwards, Kate said, "Not only did all the students in the class increase their proficiency on the standard, we had an unexpected surprise. One of our students has been numb to school all year. No matter what we did, we could not motivate him. After we introduced the acceleration center, he was so excited that he kept asking when we could do it again. We were amazed at his enthusiasm, and his assessment showed improvement. The acceleration center activity worked."

Brett and Kate started with one concept: multiplication. After implementation, they were happy with the results. Now they can add to the foundation, incorporating more activities at different levels for skills in the math strand for multiplication.

Step 11: Assess and Adjust Student Folders (see Figure 8.7)

- Does it work? If so, great!
- Does it need improvement? If it does, make the necessary adjustments.
- Does the data indicate negative gains? If so, discard it and try something else.

ACCELERATION CENTER COMPONENTS   ■

Individualized student goal charts: Each of the goal charts included in the remainder of this chapter (Figures 8.9 through 8.16, beginning on page 182) is divided into at least two sections: Have-to's and Choices. Some also add a third section: Once-A-Weekers. There are two chart levels: one for self-starters and one for students who need more support. Charts for students who need more support, especially reading support, might include illustrations, have additional required components, and have fewer optional activities. Do not reduce choices for students who need more support because choices are motivational.

   Coaching session: Coaching sessions offer teachers the opportunity to lead individuals or small groups of students in assignments appropriate to their achievement level.

   Written response journals: This component allows students the opportunity to practice written response skills required to meet state standards and written response goals for math, English, language arts, social studies, and science.

   Independent reading or study: This option provides students with the opportunity to improve reading skills and provides time to study vocabulary words, flash cards, and the like. If this option is used for study, students should use strategies based on their learning style. It would be a waste of time to have students study ineffectively. Avoid having students study by completing handouts, staring at their books, writing things three times each, or using any number of ineffective strategies that students typically use. Students who are working on reading skills should be using materials at, or just slightly above, their reading level. *It is imperative that teachers know the levels of the texts students are reading.*

Figure 8.7

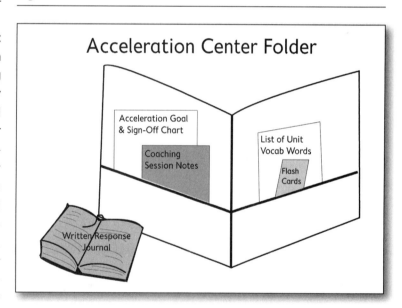

   Acceleration component: Assignment in this component is targeted to address student difficulties and accelerate student learning.

KEEP INVENTORY   ■

Recently I was doing a full-day workshop on acceleration centers, and a teacher who had been doing learning centers for many years was in the group. She said, "You forgot a piece. You must have an inventory sheet. Have students doing inventory with a checklist, or you're going to be missing parts the next time students go to do the activity." Inventory all materials, and teach your student experts to check the inventory after each session. It may be a small step, but it's an important one!

■ TIPS FOR SUCCESSFUL ACCELERATION CENTERS

- Reassign partners every four to five weeks.
- Don't change partners in response to student requests or complaints. Doing so opens up a Pandora's box of potential problems.
- Acceleration center assignments must be able to be managed and completed independently. If students cannot manage the assignments by themselves, they will often stop completely or interrupt the teachers or the other groups for help. The goal of the center is not only for students to be able to increase achievement but also for teachers to gain valuable time for conferences or uninterrupted work in small groups. Teachers must be able to optimize acceleration center time.
- Acceleration centers are not thematic, nor do they become obsolete at any point during school year. Avoid any seasonal connotation. They are designed for sustainability, requiring minimal prep work when preparation for the centers is viewed as a means of creating lesson plans suitable for an entire school year.
- Use acceleration centers to support state standards or curriculum goals, from basic to proficient.
- Create procedures and rules for utilizing acceleration centers with students as part of the process. By doing so, teachers engage students in the process, and they are more likely to buy into it.
- If setting up multiple centers, start with one and practice the rules and procedures using the first one as a teaching tool.
- As silly as it may sound to a secondary teacher, whether middle school, junior high, or high school, it is imperative to have students practice moving from their seats to the acceleration center to choose an activity and back to their seats or small groups until they can do it quietly and efficiently. This typically will take 10 or 15 minutes of practice, set up as a timed contest. Use a stopwatch and practice until students can run the procedure in three minutes or less. It may be beneficial to incorporate a reward system to maintain proper behavior and efficiency over the course of the school year.
- Keep records of completed assignments and how those assignments align to state standards or curriculum goals.
- Train one or two student experts on how the acceleration centers function. They do not need to understand the academic content of the

materials in the center; rather, they need to teach other students how to follow the instructions in the folders (see Figure 8.8), how to keep the center organized, and how to explain the logistics of the center to other students. The student expert makes it possible for students to work without interrupting the teacher while the teacher is coaching others.

Figure 8.8

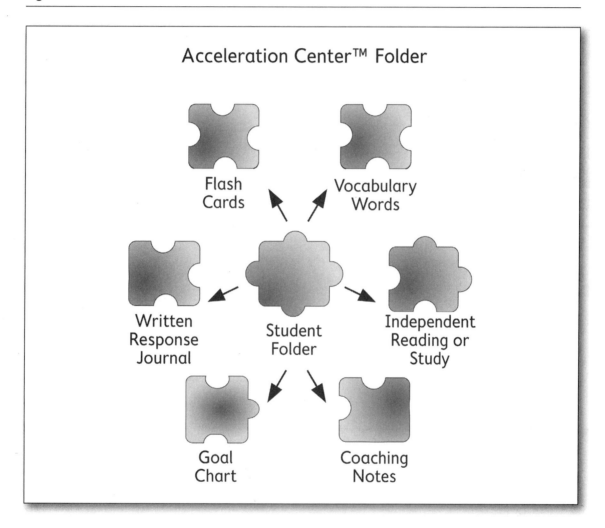

Acceleration Center™ Folder

Flash Cards

Vocabulary Words

Written Response Journal

Student Folder

Independent Reading or Study

Goal Chart

Coaching Notes

Figure 8.9 Acceleration Chart, Style 1

Acceleration Center Goal Chart & Sign-off

Name _____ Date _____

Coaching Group Name _____

Have- To's		Mon	Tue	Wed	Thu	Fri
Coaching Session						
Written Response Journal						
Test Prep (Flash cards, peer practice, Design-a-Test, etc.)						
Accelerated Component						

Once-a- Weekers	Mon	Thu	Wed	Thu	Fri
Challenge Activity or investigation					
Independent Reading or Study					

Choices (Examples)	Mon	Thu	Wed	Thu	Fri
United Streaming Video on topic					
Flashcardexchange.com or Quia.com					
Accelerated Reader					
Independent Reading on Topic					

Multi-day Chart – LS

Figure 8.10 Acceleration Chart, Variation 2

Acceleration Center Goal Chart & Sign-off

Name _____ Date _____

Coaching Group Name _____

Have-To's		Mon	Tue	Wed	Thu	Fri
Coaching Session						
Written Response Journal						
Acceleration Component						

Once-a-Weekers	Mon	Thu	Wed	Thu	Fri
Challenge Activity or investigation					
Independent Reading or Study					
Test Prep (Flash cards, peer practice, Design-a-Test, etc.)					

Choices (Examples)	Mon	Thu	Wed	Thu	Fri
United Streaming Video on topic					
Flashcardexchange.com or Quia.com					
Accelerated Reader					
Peer Tutoring					

Multi-day Chart – IL

Figure 8.11 Acceleration Chart, Variation 3

Acceleration Center Goal Chart & Sign-off

Name _____ Date _____

Coaching Group Name _____

Weekly Have- To's		Sign-off
Coaching Session		
Written Response Journal (10 min)		
Accelerated Component (10 min)		

Choices (10 min) (Examples)	Sign-off
United Streaming Video on topic	
Flashcardexchange.com or Quia.com	
Challenge Activity or investigation	
Independent Reading on Topic	
Test Prep (Flash cards, peer practice, etc.)	

Comments & Notes

Once-a-Week Chart – LS

Figure 8.12 Acceleration Chart, Variation 4

Acceleration Center Goal Chart & Sign-off

Name _____ Date _____

Coaching Group Name _____

Weekly Have- To's	Sign-off
Coaching Session (10 min)	
Acceleration Component (10 min)	

Choices (10 min) (Examples)	Sign-off
United Streaming Video on topic	
Flashcardexchange.com or Quia.com	
Challenge Activity or investigation	
Independent Reading on Topic	
Test Prep (Flash cards, peer practice, etc.)	
Written Response Journal (10 min)	

Comments & Notes

Once-a-Week Chart – IL

Figure 8.13   Acceleration Chart, Variation 5

Acceleration Center Goal Chart & Sign-off

Name _____ Date _____

Coaching Group Name _____

Have-To's		Mon	Tue	Wed	Thu	Fri
Coaching Session						
Written Response Journal						
Test Prep (Flash cards, peer practice, Design-a-Test, etc.)						
Accelerated Component						

Once-a- Weekers	Mon	Thu	Wed	Thu	Fri

Choices (Examples)	Mon	Thu	Wed	Thu	Fri

Multi-day Chart – LS

Figure 8.14 Acceleration Chart, Variation 6

Acceleration Center Goal Chart & Sign-off

Name _____ Date _____

Coaching Group Name _____

Have- To's		Mon	Tue	Wed	Thu	Fri
Coaching Session						
Written Response Journal						
Acceleration Component						

Once-a- Weekers	Mon	Thu	Wed	Thu	Fri

Choices (Examples)	Mon	Thu	Wed	Thu	Fri

Multi-day Chart – IL

Figure 8.15 Acceleration Chart, Variation 7

Acceleration Center Goal Chart & Sign-off

Name _____ Date _____

Coaching Group Name _____

Weekly Have- To's		Sign-off
Coaching Session		
Written Response Journal (10 min)		
Accelerated Component (10 min)		

Choices (10 min) (Examples)	Sign-off

Comments & Notes

Once-a-Week Chart – LS

Figure 8.16   Acceleration Chart, Variation 8

Acceleration Center Goal Chart & Sign-off

Name _____ Date _____

Coaching Group Name _____

Weekly Have- To's	Sign-off
Coaching Session (10 min)	
Acceleration Component (10 min)	

Choices (10 min) (Examples)	Sign-off

Comments & Notes

Once-a-Week Chart – IL

Concluding Thoughts

Teaching in the 21st century is both challenging and rewarding. Children learn differently than they did when we were students and when we (many of us) began teaching. Because we live in an Internet- and media-driven society, students are much more aware of the world around them than we were at their age. That awareness affects their motivation, attitudes, and their ability to relate to the curriculum. Science and research have shown that in order to succeed with our students, we must be willing to employ a variety of strategies in our classrooms to reach all learners.

This book models strategies that I *know* work in the secondary classroom. I've used them. I've witnessed them being successful. I've seen students who I thought could never reach a higher bar achieve success with the right tools, and the teachers who differentiate appropriately. With **R**eally **T**errific **I**nstruction, students focus and learn.

It is my hope that the sample lesson plans and strategies in this text will help you experience student success and the joy that comes from knowing that you've made a difference. RTI is not about making more work for you; it's about reaching all students that need what you have to offer as efficiently and completely as possible.

Enjoy, and keep making a difference!

Strategy	English	Math	Reading	Science	Social Studies	Spelling	Vocabulary	Writing	ESL
Signing					X	X	X		X
Graphic Organizers & Mind Maps	X	X	X	X	X		X	X	X
SWBS Summary	X	X	X	X	X				X
QAR	X	X	X	X	X				
Picture Books	X	X	X	X	X		X	X	
K-W-L	X	X	X	X	X		X		
Fact versus Opinion	X	X	X	X	X				
Friendly Letter	X			X	X			X	
Clustering	X			X	X			X	
Manipulatives		X		X	X				
Graphing		X		X	X				X
Sequence Strips	X	X	X	X	X				X
Analogies				X	X				
Chunking	X	X	X	X	X	X	X		X
Paraphrasing	X		X	X	X				X
Whisper It	X	X	X	X	X	X	X	X	X
If/Then Rulebook	X	X	X			X	X	X	X
Similarities & Differences	X			X	X				X
Summarizing	X	X	X	X	X			X	X
Questioning	X	X		X	X				X

Bibliography

Ausubel, D. P. (1963). *The psychology of meaningful verbal learning: An introduction to school learning*. New York: Grune & Statton.

Barba, R. H., & Merchant, L. J. (1990). The effects of embedding generative cognitive strategies in science software. *Journal of Computers in Mathematics and Science Teaching, 10*(1), 59–65.

Bell, F. (2005). *Total body learning: Movement and academics*. Manchester, NH: Cogent Catalyst.

Bender, W., & Shores, C. (2007). *Response to intervention: A practical guide for every teacher*. Thousand Oaks, CA: Corwin.

Bickmore, S. B. J., & Hundley, M. (2001). Picture books for young adult readers. *The Alan Review, 28*(3).

Brown-Chidsey, R., & Steege, M. W. (2005). *Response to intervention: Principles and strategies for effective practice*. New York: Guilford Press.

Burns, P. C., Roe, B. D., & Smith, S. (2009). *Teaching reading in today's elementary schools* (8th ed.). Florence, KY: Cengage Learning.

Cebulla, G. (2000). *Improving student achievement in mathematics*. Switzerland: International Academy of Education and International Bureau of Education.

Cisneros, S. (1984). *The house on Mango Street*. Houston, TX: Arte Público Press.

Connery, K. F. (2007). Graphing predictions. *The Science Teacher, 74*(2), 42–46.

Daniels, M. (Ed.). (2001). *Dancing with words: Signing for hearing children's literacy*. Westport, CT: Bergin & Garvey.

Ehren, B. J. (2000). Mnemonic devices. Retrieved from http://www2.ku.edu/~onlineacademy/academymodules/a304/support/xpages/a304b0_20600.html.

Ewy, C. A. (2003). *Teaching with visual frameworks: Focused learning and achievement through instructional graphics co-created by students and teachers*. Thousand Oaks, CA: Corwin.

Fitzell, S. G., & Fitzell, S. (2006). *Umm . . . studying? What's that? Learning strategies for the overwhelmed and confused college and high school student*. Manchester, NH: Cogent Catalyst.

Fitzell, S. G. (2010). *Memorization and test taking strategies for the differentiated, inclusive and RTI classroom* [video]. Available from http://www.cogentcatalyst.com/audio-and-video/memorization-and-test-taking-strategies/.

Fox, D. L., & Short, K. G. (2003). *Stories matter: The complexity of cultural authenticity in children's literature*. Urbana, IL: National Council of Teachers of English.

Friedel, A. W., Gabel, D. I., & Samuel, J. (1990). Using analogs for chemistry problem solving: Does it increase understanding? *School Science and Mathematics, 90*, 674–682.

Furukawa, J. (1978, August). *Chunking method of teaching and studying: II*. Paper presented at the meeting of the American Psychological Association, Toronto, CA. Retrieved from http://www.eric.ed.gov/ERICWebPortal/search/detailmini.jsp?_nfpb=true&_&ERICExtSearch_SearchValue_0=ED165097&ERICExtSearch_SearchType_0=no&accno=ED165097.

Gick, M. L., & Holyoak, K. (1983). Schema induction and analogical transfer. *Cognitive Psychology, 15*, 138.

Gregory, G. (2008). *Differentiated instructional strategies in practice: Training, implementation, and supervision* (2nd ed.). Thousand Oaks, CA: Corwin.

Grigg, W. S., Lauko, M. A., & Brockway, D. M. (2006). *The nation's report card: Science 2005* (NCES 2006–466). U.S. Department of Education, National Center for Education Statistics. Washington, DC: U.S. Government Printing Office.

Grouws, D. A., & Cebulla, K. J. (2000). *Improving student achievement in mathematics.* Paper presented at the International Academy of Education. Retrieved from http://www.ibe.unesco.org/publications/educationalpracticesseriespdf/prac04e.pdf.

Gunning, T. G. (2008). *Developing higher-level literacy in all students: Building reading, reasoning, and responding.* Boston: Allyn & Bacon.

Hadaway, N. L., & Mundy, J. (1999). Children's informational picture books visit a secondary ESL classroom. *Journal of Adolescent & Adult Literacy, 42*(6), 464–476.

Hall, S. L. (2008). *Implementing Response to Intervention: A principal's guide.* Thousand Oaks, CA: Corwin.

Hanson, H. M. (Director). (2009). *RTI and DI: Response to Intervention and Differentiated Instruction* [DVD]. Port Chester, NY: National Professional Resources. Available at http://www.nprinc.com/rti/drtd.htm.

Harvey, S., & Goudvis, A. (2007). *Strategies that work: Teaching comprehension for understanding and engagement.* Portland, ME: Stenhouse Publishers.

Hoff, R. (1988). *I can see you naked: A fearless guide to making great presentations.* Kansas City, MO: Andrews & McMeel.

Hyerle, D. (2009). *Visual tools for transforming information into knowledge* (2nd ed.). Thousand Oaks, CA: Corwin.

James, I., & Carter, T. S. (2007). Questioning and informational texts: Scaffolding students comprehension of content areas. *Forum on Public Policy: A Journal of the Oxford Round Table.* Retrieved from http://www.forumonpublicpolicy.com/archivesum07/james.rev.pdf.

Johnson, N. J., & Giorgis., C. (Eds.). (2007). *The wonder of it all: When literature and literacy intersect.* Portsmouth, NH: Heinemann.

Kellogg, S. (1985). *Chicken Little.* New York: HarperCollins.

Koehler, L. J. S., & Lloyd, L. L. (1986, September). *Using fingerspelling/manual signs to facilitate reading and spelling.* Paper presented at the Biennial Conference of the International Society for Augmentative and Alternative Communication, Cardiff, UK.

Lederer, J. M. (2000). Reciprocal teaching of social studies in inclusive elementary classrooms. *Journal of Learning Disabilities, 33*(1), 91–106.

Levine, D. M. (2003). *A mind at a time.* New York: Simon and Schuster.

Marzano, R. J., Paynter, D. E, Kendall, J. S., Pickering, D., & Marzano, L. (1991). *Literacy plus: An integrated approach to teaching reading, writing, vocabulary, and reasoning (teacher's guide).* Columbus, OH: Zaner-Bloser.

Marzano, R. J., Pickering, D. J., & Pollock, J. E. (2001). *Classroom instruction that works: Research-based strategies for increasing student achievement.* Alexandria, VA: Association for Supervision and Curriculum Development.

Math Learning Center. (2005–2011). *Math and the mind's eye* (Units 1–14). Retrieved from http://www.mathlearningcenter.org/curriculum/highschool/minds-eye.

Miller, G. A. (1956). The magical number seven, plus or minus two: Some limits on our capacity for processing information. *Psychological Review, 63*, 81–97.

Moore, D. W., & Readence, J. E. (1984). A quantitative and qualitative review of graphic organizer research. *Journal of Educational Research, 78*, 11–17.

National Center for History in the Schools. (1996). *National standards for history, revised edition.* Los Angeles, CA: Author.

National Reading Panel. (2000). *Teaching children to read: An evidence-based assessment of the scientific research literature on reading and its implications for reading instruction* (Report). Washington, DC: National Institute of Child Health and Human Development.

Neuschwander, C. (1999–2009). *Sir Cumference* [complete series]. Watertown, MA: Charlesbridge.

Nilson, L. B. (1998). *Teaching at its best : A research-based resource for college instructors.* Bolton, MA: Anker.

Oczkus, L. D. (2003). *Reciprocal teaching at work: Strategies for improving reading comprehension.* Newark, DE: International Reading Association.

O'Donnell, A. M., & King, A. (1999). *Cognitive perspectives on peer learning.* Mahwah, NJ: Lawrence Erlbaum.

Opitz, M., Rubin, D., & Erekson, J. (2011). *Reading diagnosis and improvement: Assessment and instruction* (7th ed.). Boston: Allyn & Bacon.

Osborn, S. (2001). Picture books for young adult readers. *The ALAN Review, 28*(3). Retrieved from http://scholar.lib.vt.edu/ejournals/ALAN/v28n3/osborn.html.

Pehrsson, R. S., & Denner, P. R. (1989). *Semantic organizers: A study strategy for special needs learners.* Rockville, MD: Aspen.

Peterson, P. (Ed.). (2007). *Hands on literacy.* Bloomington, IN: AuthorHouse.

Picciotto, H. (1998). Operation sense, tool-based pedagogy, curricular breadth: A proposal. Retrieved from http://www.mathedpage.org/annotated-map.html#manipulatives.

Picciotto, H. (2010). Algebra manipulatives: Comparison and history. San Francisco: Henri Picciotto. Retrieved March 6, 2010, from http://www.MathEdPage.org/manipulatives/alg-manip.html

Picciotto, H. (n.d.). Algebra manipulatives: Comparison and history. Retrieved from http://www.MathEdPage.org/manipulatives/alg-manip.html.

Polacco, P. (2000). *The butterfly.* New York: Puffin Books.

Prinz, P., & Strong, M. (1995, July). The interrelationship among cognition, sign language, and literacy. Paper presented at the 18th International Conference on Education of the Deaf. Tel-Aviv, Israel.

Prinz, P., & Strong, M. (1997). A study of the relationship between American Sign Language and English literacy. *Journal of Deaf Studies and Deaf Education, 2*(1), 37–46.

Raphael, T., Highfield, K., & Au, K. H. (2006). *QAR now: A powerful and practical framework that develops comprehension and higher-level thinking in all students (theory and practice).* New York: Scholastic Press.

Rasinski, T. V. (2003). *The fluent reader: Oral reading strategies for building word recognition, fluency, and comprehension.* New York: Scholastic Press.

Reys, R. E., Lindquist, M. M., Lambdin, D. V., Suydam, M. N., & Smith, N. (2009). *Helping children learn mathematics* (9th ed.). Englewood Cliffs, NJ: Prentice Hall.

Ringgold, F. (1991). *Tar Beach.* New York: Crown.

Robinson, B. (2007, April 10). *Using picture books to teach literary terms in the high school English classroom.* Asheville: University of North Carolina–Asheville. Available at http://facstaff.unca.edu/mcglinn/Bridget%20PP%202.ppt.

Rule, A. C., & Furletti, Charles. (2004). Using form and function analogy object boxes to teach human body systems. *School Science and Mathematics, 104*(8), 155–169.

Scieszka, J. (1994). *The Frog Prince, continued.* New York: Puffin Books.

Scieszka, J. (2004). *Science verse.* New York: Penguin.

Shores, C., & Chester, K. (2009). *Using RTI for school improvement: Raising every student's achievement scores.* Thousand Oaks, CA: Corwin.

Shugarman, S. L., & Hurst, J. B. (1986). Purposeful paraphrasing: Promoting a nontrivial pursuit for meaning. *Journal of Reading, 29*(5), 396–399.

Smith, L. (1996). *The happy Hocky family.* New York: Puffin Books.

Snapp, J. C., & Glover, J. A. (1990). Advance organizers and study questions. *Journal of Educational Research, 83*(5), 266–271.

Spandel, V., & Culham, R. (1994). *An annotated bibliography for use with the 6-trait analytic model of writing assessment and instruction.* Portland, OR: Northwest Regional Education Laboratory.

Steig, W. (1998). *Sylvester and the magic pebble.* New York: Simon & Schuster.

Strange, C. (1996). *Collector's guide to Tinker Toys*. Paducah, KY: Collector Books.

Tierney, R. J., Soter, A., O'Flahavan, J. F., & McGinley, W. (1989). The effects of reading and writing upon thinking critically. *Reading Research Quarterly, 24*(2), 134–173.

Turner, A. (1987). *Nettie's trip south*. New York: Simon & Schuster.

Van Allsburg, C. (1986). *The stranger*. Boston: Houghton Mifflin.

Witzel, B. S. (2005). Using CRA to teach algebra to students with math difficulties in inclusive settings. *Learning Disabilities: A Contemporary Journal, 3*(2), 49–60.

Witzel, B. S. (2007). Algebra interventions for students who struggle. Retrieved from http://www.centeroninstruction.org/files/Witzel%20presentation%2Eppt.

Witzel, B. S., & Riccomini, P. J. (2010). *Solving equations: An algebra intervention*. Boston: Allyn & Bacon.

Wong, P. W., & Brizuela, B. (2006). *Everest trek*. Portland, ME: Walch.

Wong, P. W., & Brizuela, B. (2007a). *Amazon mission*. Portland, ME: Walch.

Wong, P. W., & Brizuela, B. (2007b). *Stranded!* Portland, ME: Walch.

Wright, J. (2007). *RTI toolkit: A practical guide for schools*. Port Chester, NY: Dude.

Yolen, J. (1993). *All those secrets of the world*. Boston: Little, Brown.

Index

CORWIN

A SAGE Company

The Corwin logo—a raven striding across an open book—represents the union of courage and learning. Corwin is committed to improving education for all learners by publishing books and other professional development resources for those serving the field of PreK–12 education. By providing practical, hands-on materials, Corwin continues to carry out the promise of its motto: **"Helping Educators Do Their Work Better."**